AF231252

First published in 2017

Published by Magwitch Books, Hastings, East Sussex

ISBN 978-0-9957923-0-2

ROGER HOPGOOD

The Image Awry

THIS BRIC-A-BRAC ENGLAND

Photographs are often seen as 'windows' on the world, giving viewers direct access to some other time and place. In treating photographs like windows we tend to forget that what they depict appears only there and nowhere else. Despite appearances, realism in photographs is nothing like reality seen by natural eyesight. For example, blurring in photographs is commonplace and it does not spoil their realism, whereas normal eyesight is not blurred. Photographic realism may be conventional and unlike the reality of eyesight, but it is supposed to honour an imaginary contract between the real world and its representation. At least, that is the case in portrait photography or photojournalism. The only groups who wilfully break the contract, and pay no penalty, are those artists who do not claim to depict the world as it appears.

Roger Hopgood adds one realistic image to another to produce a visual puzzle. Whereas portraiture and news photographs are supposed to match expectations of 'being there', Hopgood's pictures deny the normal 'window' function of the medium. Instead, small objects are made large and float in (or above) the landscape. These objects are either flat or occupy a very shallow space, whereas the landscapes are often deep, with horizons some way off. The eye is drawn to the landscape but the view is obstructed, often by brightly lit, kitsch or gimcrack objects. Why are they conjoined in this fashion? Are the two parts of the image just placed in some jocular or pointed opposition, such as a natural landscape with a cheap, transfer-printed plate of huntsmen and hounds? Clearly, the unsympathetic objects that hover in the foreground do indeed contrast with the views they obscure.

Their differences are emphatic, but that does not make them absolute. To the contrary, both the land underfoot and the (apparently) air-borne bric-a-brac are somewhat shabby, despite their being shaped if not manufactured. Most of the landscapes are obviously cultivated, and even brooks and seashores are not free of management. The houses, crops, and fields may differ in scale and import from the spoons, penknives, gewgaws (and so on) but they belong to the same economy of usage and idealisation. Everything that appears here is used, elsewhere, to embody, replicate or enthuse a narrative of Englishness: an old world of cottages and sweet maids, horses and hounds, smithies and country craft that somehow overlay one another in the mythic idea of an intimate 'England' of fellowship. The mythic country is always integrated.

Roger Hopgood's photographs allow all those ideas to surface, but nothing rests exactly where convention says it should. The milkmaid, hunters, brasses and so forth should be comfortable, quiescent or even dead metaphors, but everything is unsettled. Everything strikes a false note - since nothing is a satisfying representation of the thing it claims to represent - not maid or hunters, not cooked meat or pots and pans; not the landscapes, which are scrubby and indefinite. Perhaps everything begins with a false note because that is the strange (but normalised) state of the country? Nothing escapes falsification. All the ordinary and overlooked landscapes and all the mass-produced objects contribute to the continuing, falsifying myth of 'England', its past and its difference from others.

Moreover, the abundance of the falsifications has always been thus. The number and concentration of false notes that make the hymn of the country signal the permanence of this myth, which is impervious to lived experience and yet touches it profoundly. Indeed, the particular mythic nature of ''England' suggests it has always been rising into falsification. The country rises into falsification because that state best represents its history. Its fate has always been to be falling away from a lost and idealised beginning and always to be rising, by falsification, into what it has become. Photographs, which are so different from natural eyesight, even when they claim to be realistic, are the perfect medium for picturing this falsification. They may be said to embody it. Consequently, whether a photograph is an authentic 'documentary' (as in the 'window' usage), or one of Hopgood's 'Treasures', each of them begins in falsification

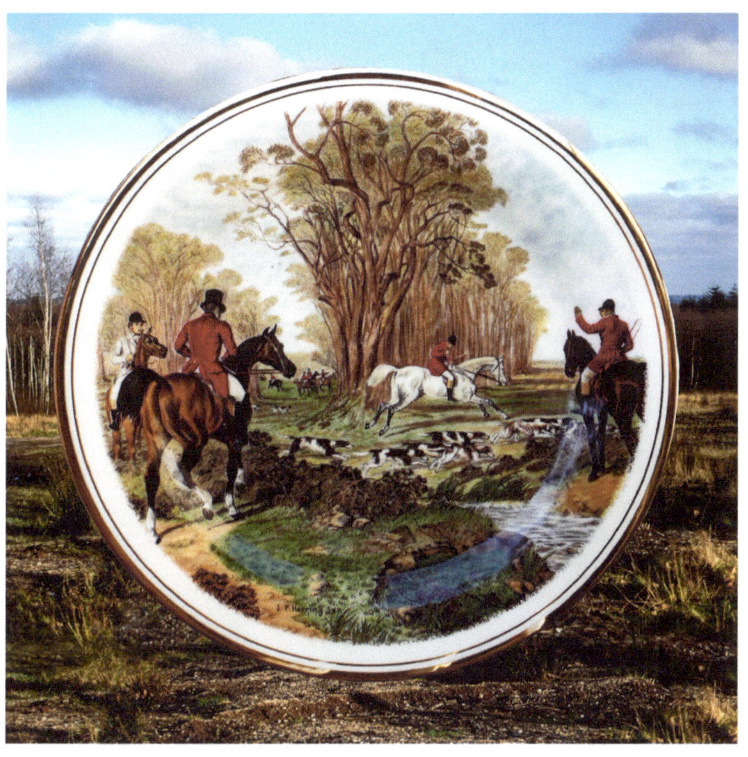

Hunting Plate, 2003
from the series *Treasures*

and manipulation. All 'realistic' images try to erase their origins as a medium and present themselves as the thing itself. Myth is similarly adamant in laying claim to deeper truths. At the same time as culture is made to seem like nature, Hopgood moves in a different direction. He cannot prevent culture turning (via myth) into nature, or normality. But he does turn the process of falsification, which is inherent in nationalism, into a different kind of virtue.

John Taylor

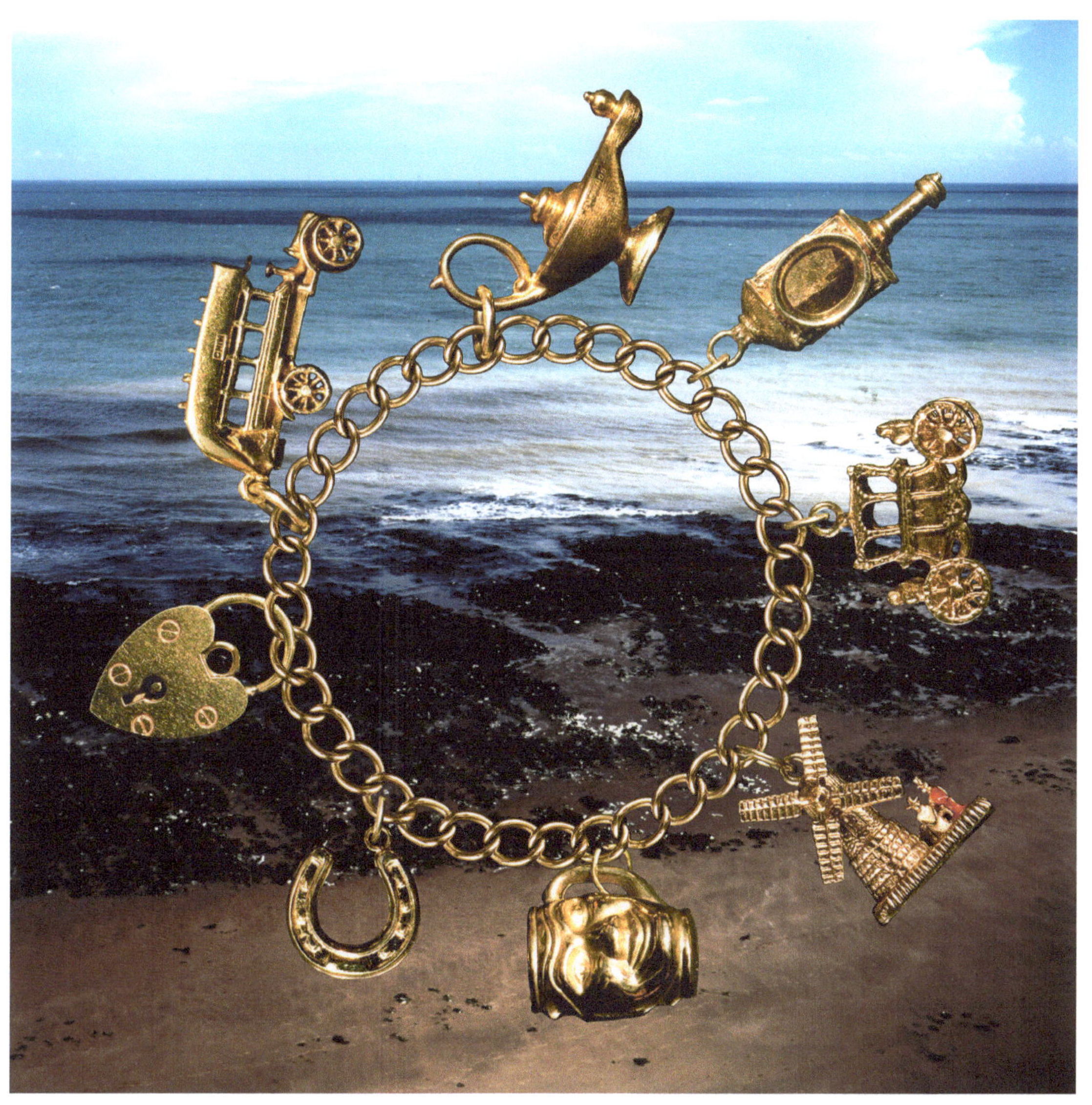

Couple (2000)
from the series *Treasures*

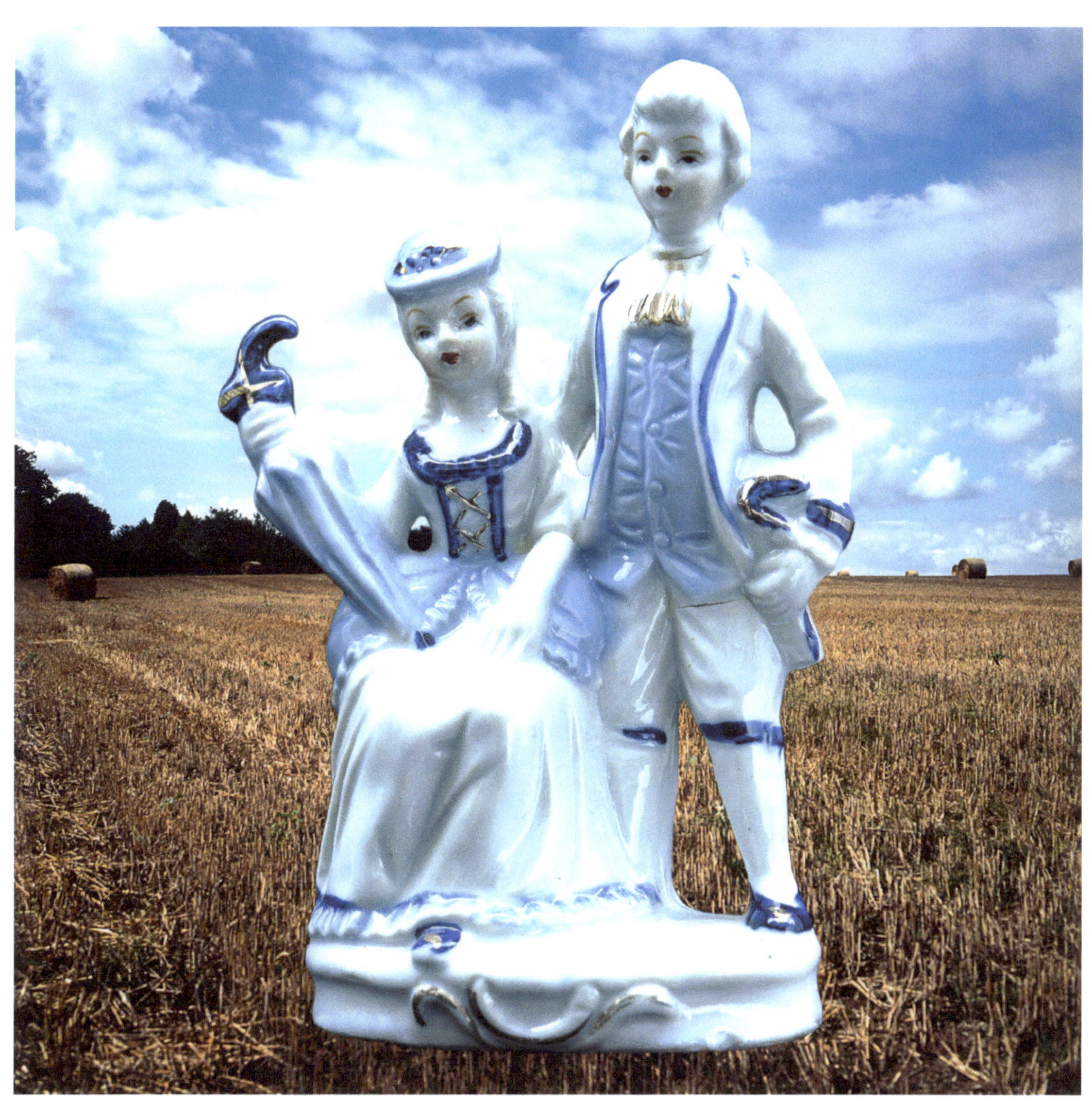

Penknives (2003)
from the series *Treasures*

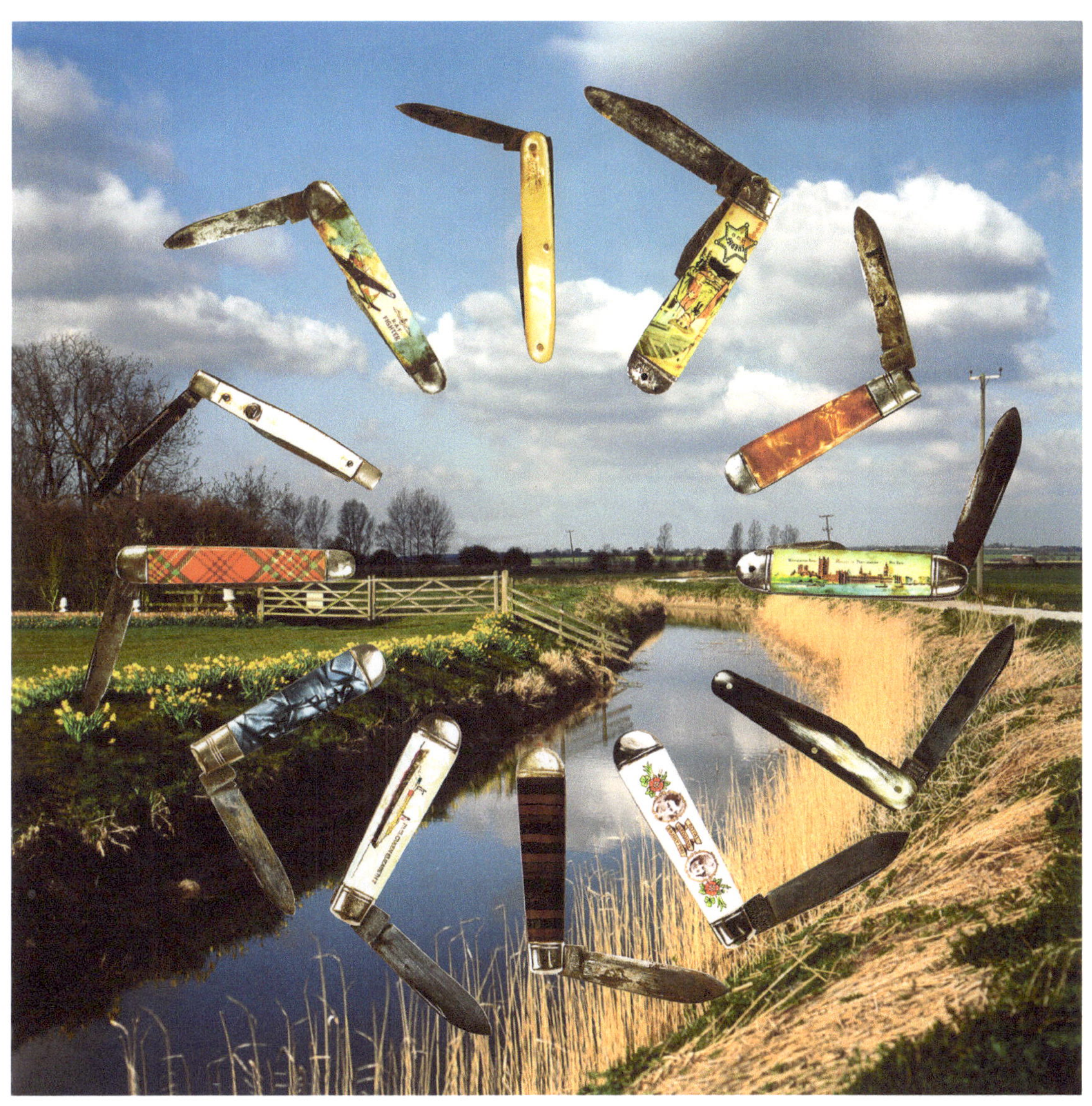

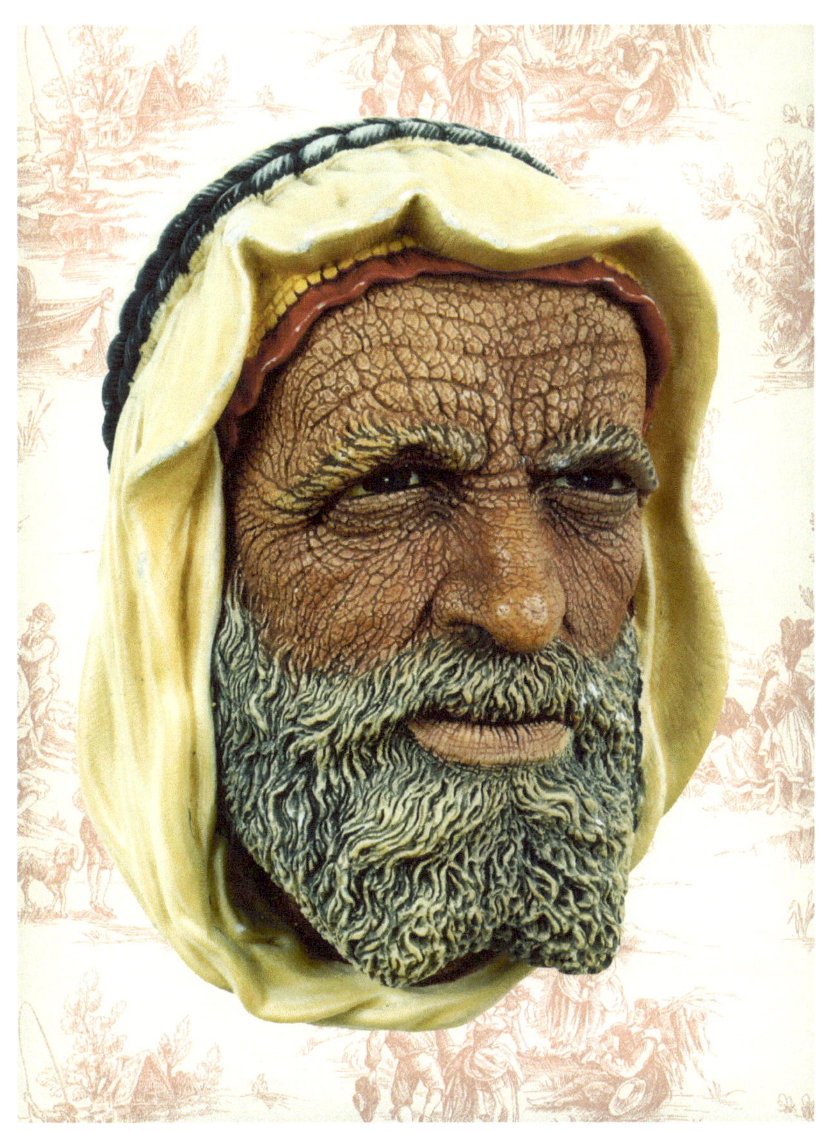

Broken Plate I (2014)
from the series *Broken Plates*

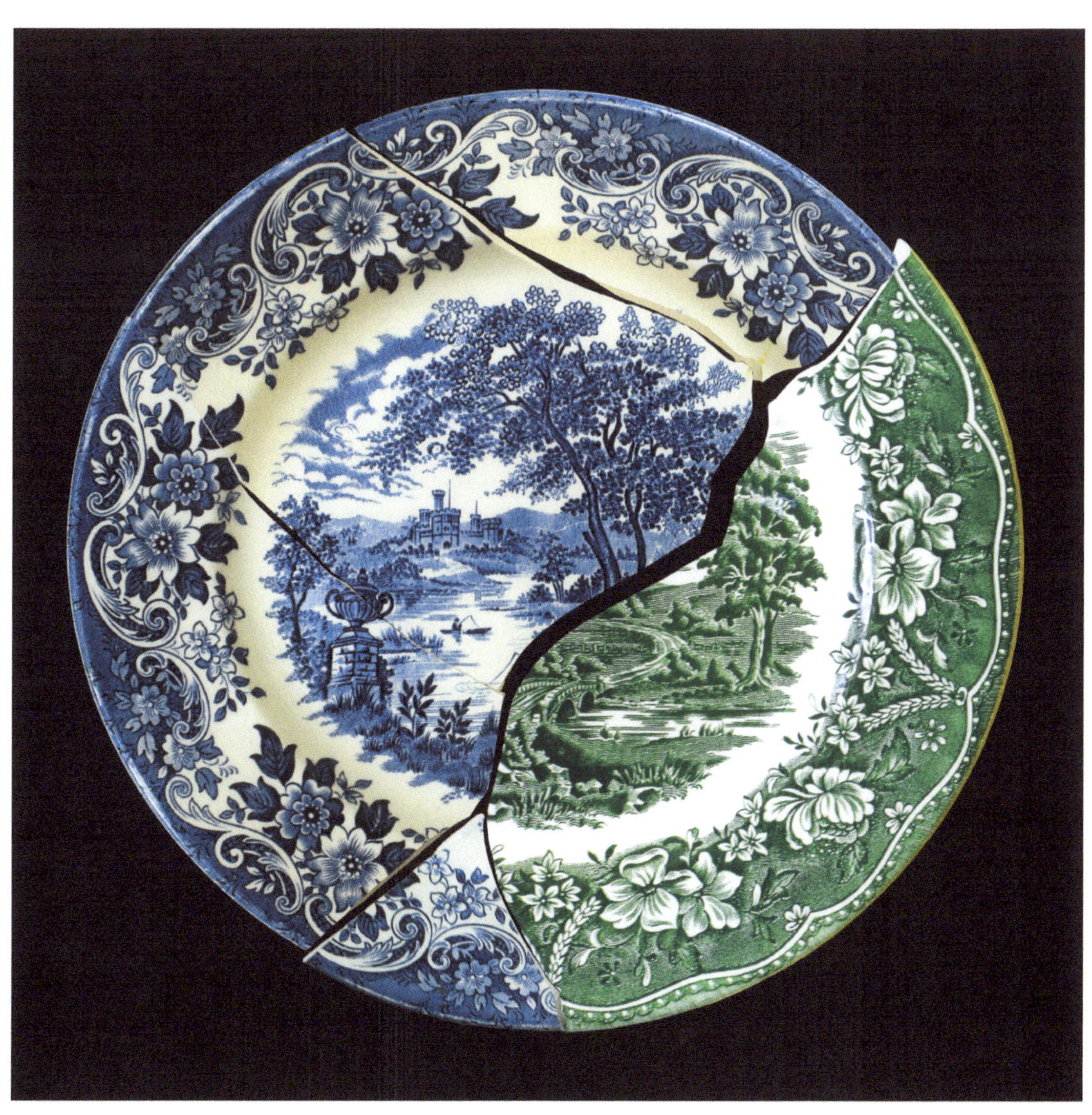

CONSTRUCTED LANDSCAPES

Landscape photography, much like the tradition within painting, presents us with a composed and conventionalised picture of the countryside as though it were evidence of something elementary, something external to human invention. Of course, this is not always the case. Debates and creative practices interrogating the nature of landscape have moved us on, and the archetypal landscape of hills and lakes, hemmed in by side-screens of arching trees and ruinous forms, have been corralled together into the category of cliché. For some, this is an irrelevance and such landscapes remain affirmative of something deeply important. For others, however, such photographs are facile confection and an anathema to serious photographic practice. Indeed, we might say that within contemporary engagements with landscape, it is the deadpan style that now rules supreme.

Yet even among those of us who see the cliché for what it is, it is hard to deny that the invocation of nature as a timeless idyll is difficult to resist. Its invitation to romanticise the view, to simultaneously look inward as well as outward, is compelling. Our general susceptibility to this is seemingly proven by the plethora of such visual expressions that still surround us in current day media culture. In such places as birthday cards, screensavers, food packaging, and a whole range of TV genres, the guilty pleasure of the picturesque lives on.

It is at this confluence of the reasoned grasp of the mapped cultural terrain and the lingering desire for the romantic landscape that the body of work in *The Image Awry* declares its meaning. The images speak of the way in which landscape is imbued with cultural resonances – national identity, collective memory, social division and exclusion – yet remains an irrepressible force in the realm of the imaginary. Landscape, we might say, is nebulous. Like a rainbow, it can never be reached, disappearing as one approaches it. In reading the work, we might immediately connect the employment of digital construction (through which these non-actual landscapes are brought into being) with a disre-gard for *genius loci* – the sense of place that drives a poetic purview of physical terrain.

In the work, cherished landscapes are something to be quantified in the same way that an ethnographer might decode a totemic artefact. Of more interest than the perceived natural beauty are the mental processes that endlessly resuscitate the romantic landscape, and keep it entwined with desire and an affirmation of self. Turning for instance to the series *Landscape with Ruin*, which features abandoned and dilapidated petrol stations, the ruinous beauty that is presented to us feels a little tainted when we learn that these are digital constructs. Nonetheless, the allusion to ruin as a motif within picturesque landscape remains affecting. As far back as the 18th century, the ruin was felt to be evocative of nature as a reclaiming force, with a pleasing melancholy being found in nature's eventual annulment of all human endeavour.

The 'gas station', in contrast in this, took on an entirely different meaning during its emergence as a cultural symbol. Long before anxiety over toxic by-products and diminishing oil reserves, the gas station was a potent signifier of freedom. This use of the gas station is easily found in Hollywood cinema but a more unusual treatment of the filling station and the freedom it offered is found in Shell's television advertising campaign of the 1950s, where the poet John Betjeman spoke of the pleasures of exploring the British countryside with the aid of Shell's network of fuel stops. Shell also funded a series of tour guides, which a number of renowned artists and writers (including Betjemen) contributed to.

In the current day, such an optimistic, view of motoring has passed. In addition to anxieties over costly, non-sustainable energy use, a streamlining of the industry has placed many filling stations beyond the point of economic viability and the gas station ruin is now a not uncommon sight. In the series, a digital transplanting of the ruins to a remoter landscape links their meaning to the original picturesque motif.

Perhaps ultimately they signify that an era is reaching its end and the technology of oil powered transportation may soon be viewed with romantic affection.

In the *Climbing Frames* series, there is a suggestion of the rural environment being invaded by structures from the inner city. The climbing frames, each shaped as a form of transport, are rusting and antiquated and seem slightly at odds with their countryside setting. In actuality, the frames were photographed in urban environments (mainly London) and digitally transferred to the fields and villages of Kent. Such forms of recreation are probably a familiar sight to anyone who grew up in the 1960s and 70s and spent their time in municipal play areas of the British townscape. Now eradicated from the more safety-conscious playgrounds of today, the tubular steel frames of the postwar years have been condemned to history, relics of the past that encapsulate an earlier, perhaps more innocent, perception of the world.

In their day, the steel-framed jet planes and rocket ships offered fantasies of escape and adventure. The ability of children to use the frames to play out narratives drawn from movies and television could be said to reveal the powers of youthful imagination, given that many of the inner-city areas where the frames were located were far less expressive of escape and 'open road' opportunity. For many working class Londoners, the Kent countryside was an achievable place of escape, but often only as a temporary one: for many, the yearly exodus to the hop farms of Kent served as an enjoyable working holiday.

Paradoxically, many of the movies fuelling ideas of escape and adventure were rooted in a sense of protection and exclusion. British sci-fi movies of the postwar years have been linked to a fear of outside threats. Movies such as *Quatermass II* (1957) and *Children of the Damned* (1964) point to anxieties over changes taking place in the modern world: a fear that technology or immigration might bring about irre-

vocable change to life within the green and pleasant land. Allusion to Otherness in cinematic narrative is found also in the *Bosson Heads* series. Here a peculiar form of bric-a-brac object, speaks of a landscape of exotic fantasy. Intricately modelled plaster wall plaques, popular in British homes in the 1960s and 70s, depict the heads of national and ethnic types such as 'Syrian' and 'Kurd', and their manufacture was likely to have taken imspiration from the exotic alterity found in movies such as *Lawrence of Arabia* (1962).

Science fiction and invisible barriers in the landscape are brought to mind in a later body of work entitled *3G Hinterland*, which probes the dead zones in the cell phone network. The videos and photographs that make up this series represent actual rather than invented landscapes, but the preoccupation with dead zones, where even a simple call on a cell phone cannot be made, conjures up an idea of rural enclaves under threat from external forces.

The work provides a survey of the 'remoter' regions of the English landscape at the end of the 3G era – anticipating subsequent waves of cell phone technologies that will eventually lead to full UK signal coverage. As well as putting us in mind of science fiction, the work connects with ideas of early landscape painting. The original Picturesque movement of the 18th century has been discussed as a reaction to the industrial revolution, and this conception of picturesque as anti-industrial and resistant to change can be traced through to present day photographic forms. Images of the dead zone environs express an atmosphere of 'wilderness' but at the same time mark out topographical information – the tracts of land where the communications infrastructure is in need of improvement. In the work, the dead zones take on an almost mystical significance as areas where technological communication breaks down and some kind of alternative state seems to be represented. In this way, although the work avoids digital construction, it remains a coherent part of a larger oeuvre where landscape is treated as mythical, divisive, yet somehow irresistable.

Caravan (2004)
from the series *Climbing Frames*

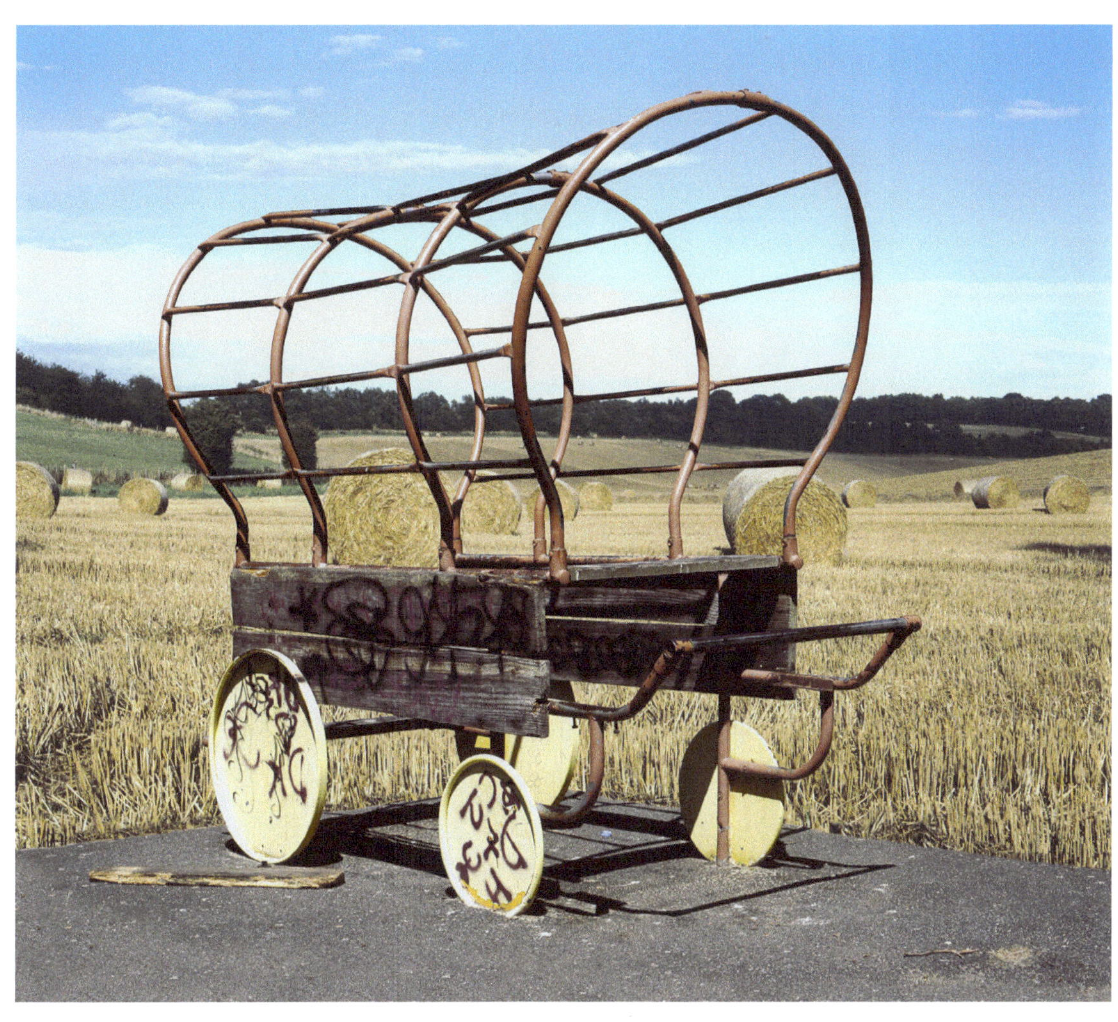

Lorry (2007)
from the series *Climbing Frames*

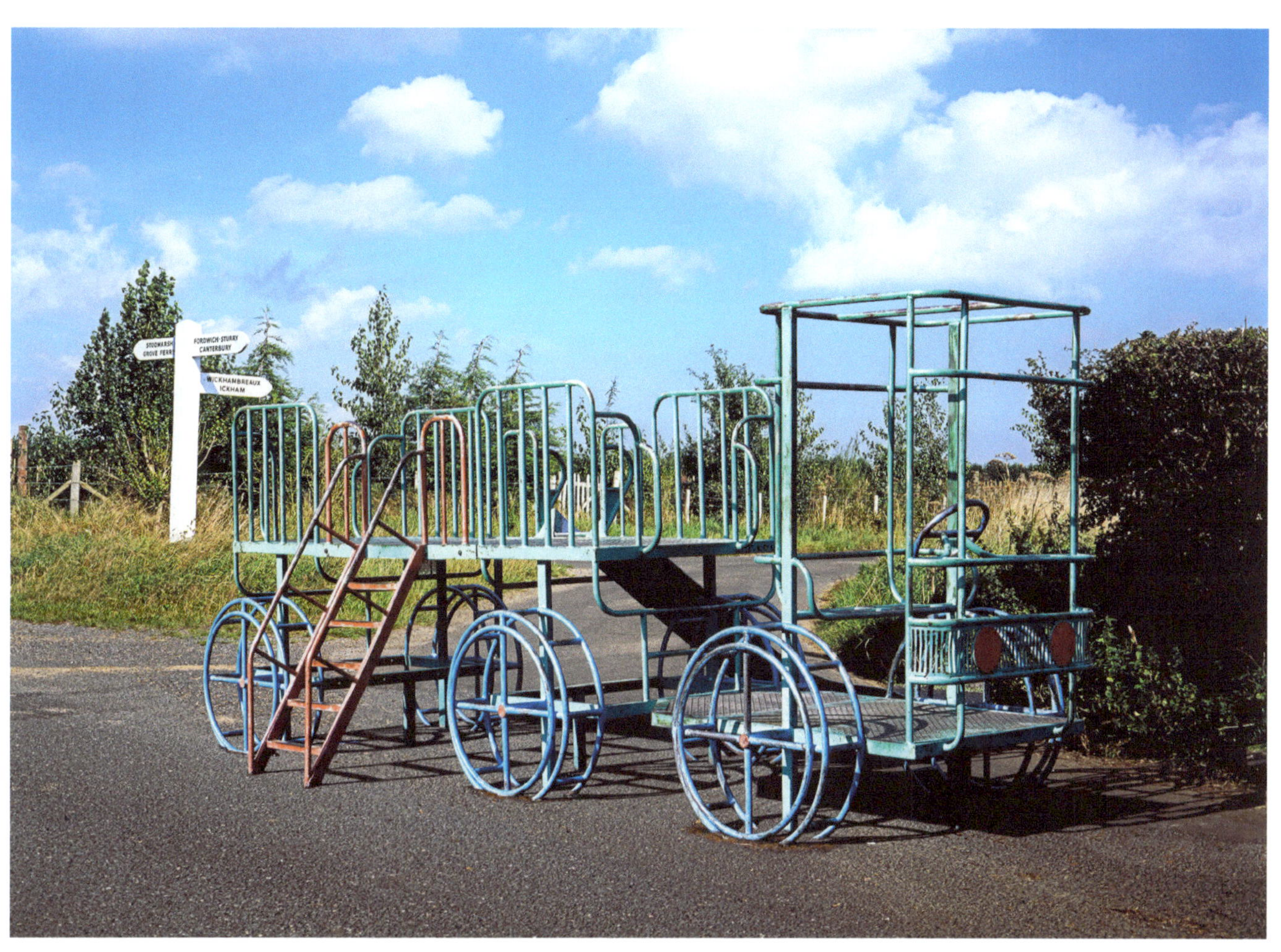
STODMARSH
GROVE FERRY
FORDWICH·STURRY
CANTERBURY
WICKHAMBREAUX
ICKHAM

Flying Saucer (2008)
from the series *Climbing Frames*

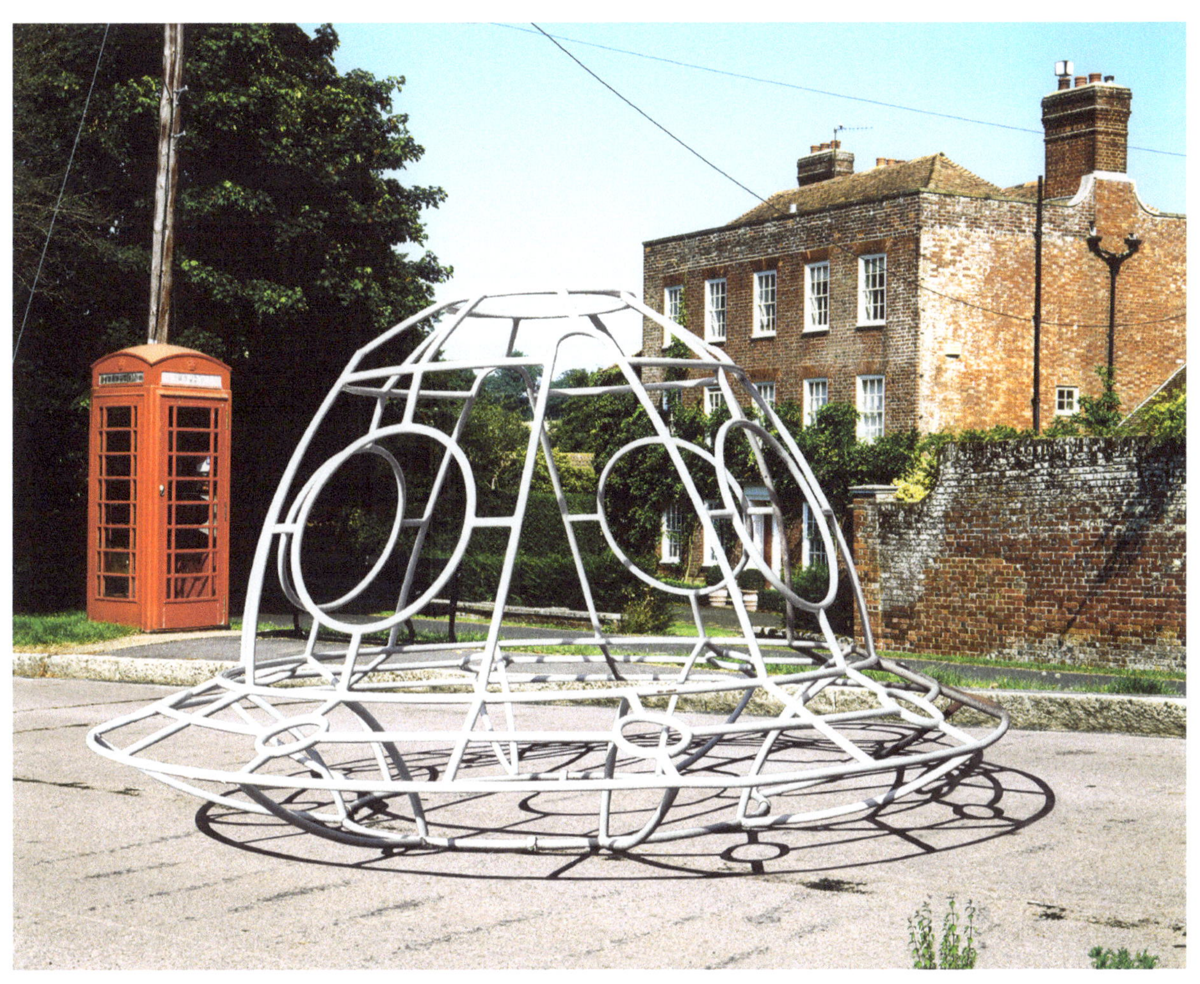

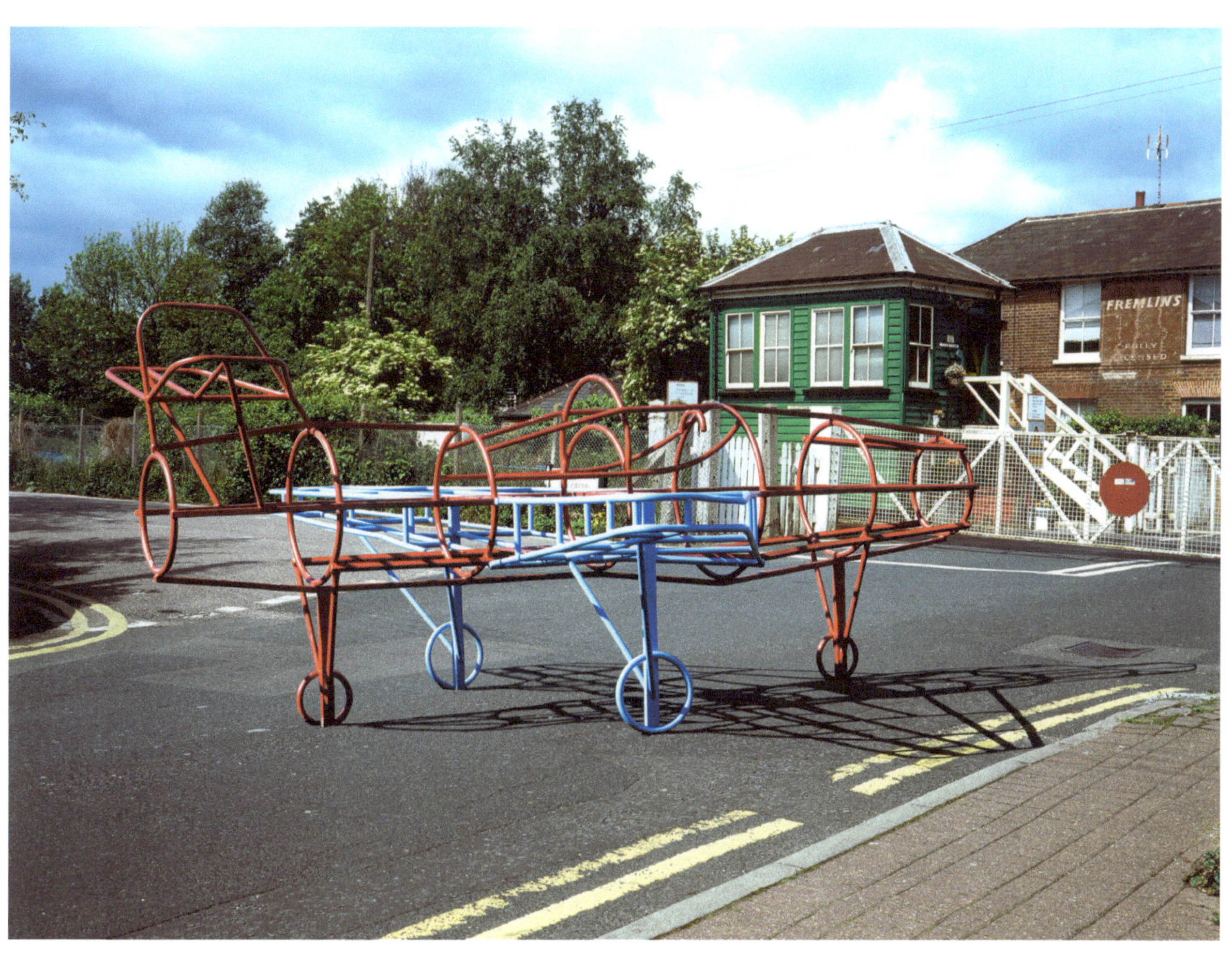

FREMLINS
FULLY
LICENSED

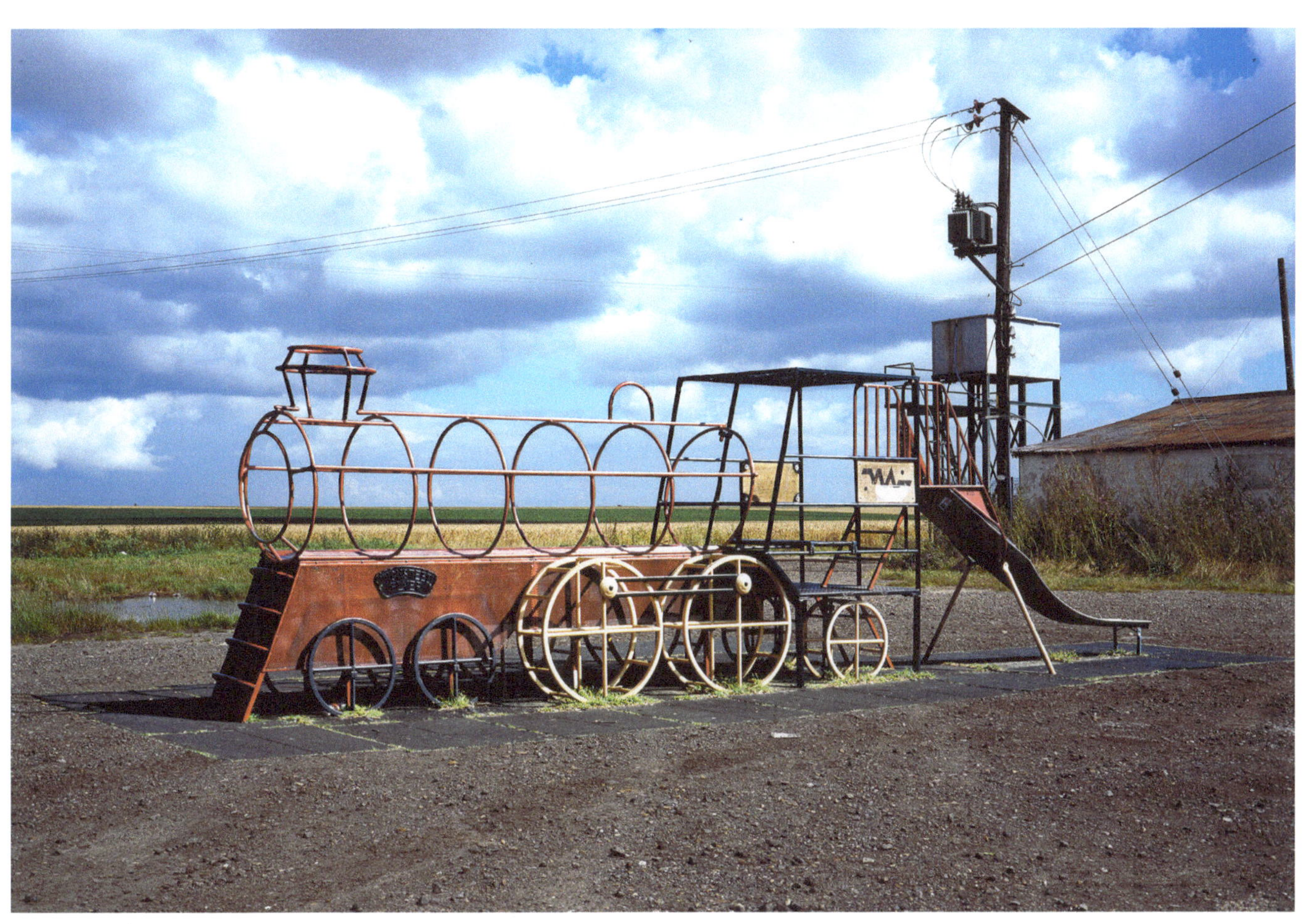

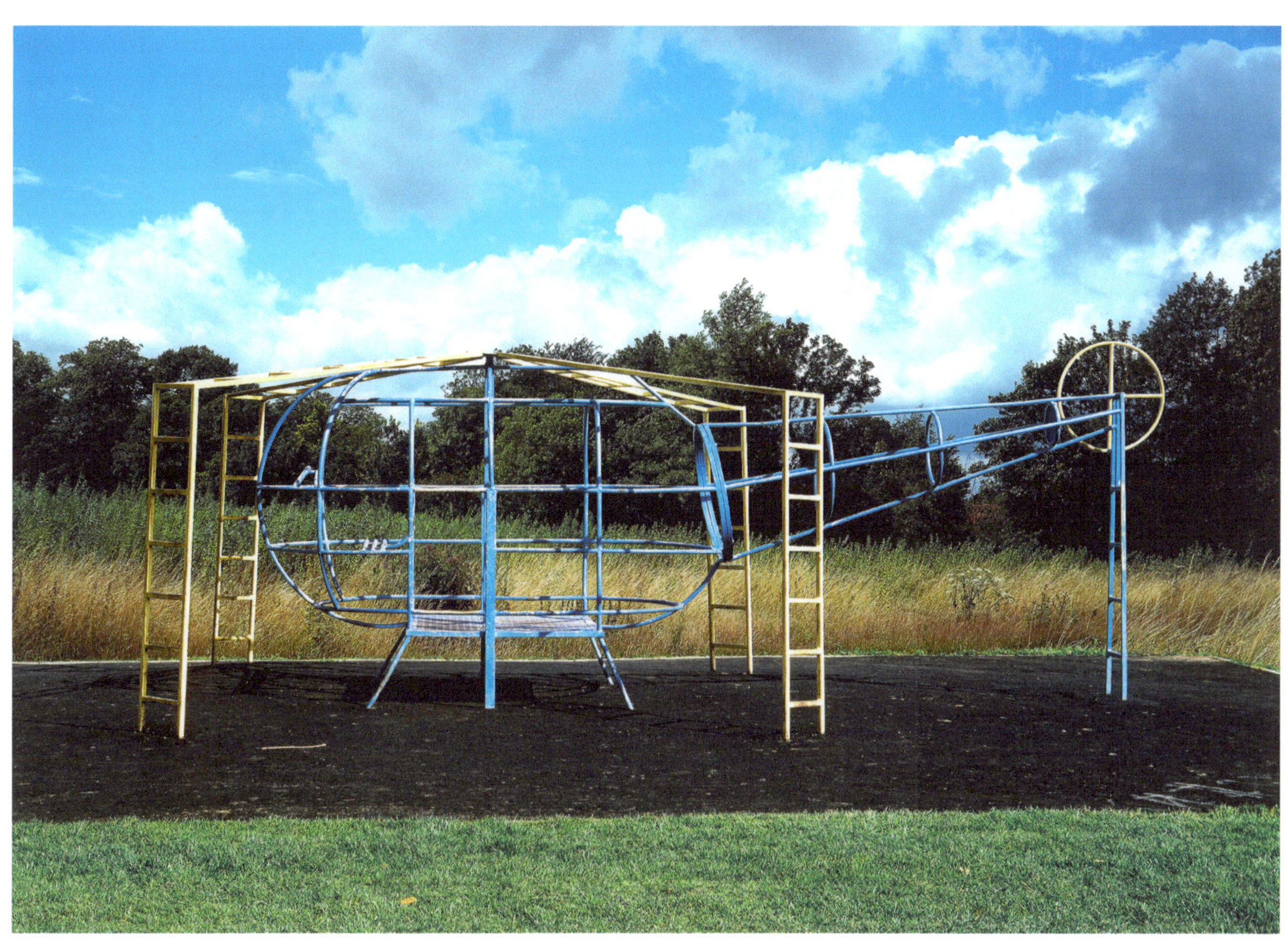

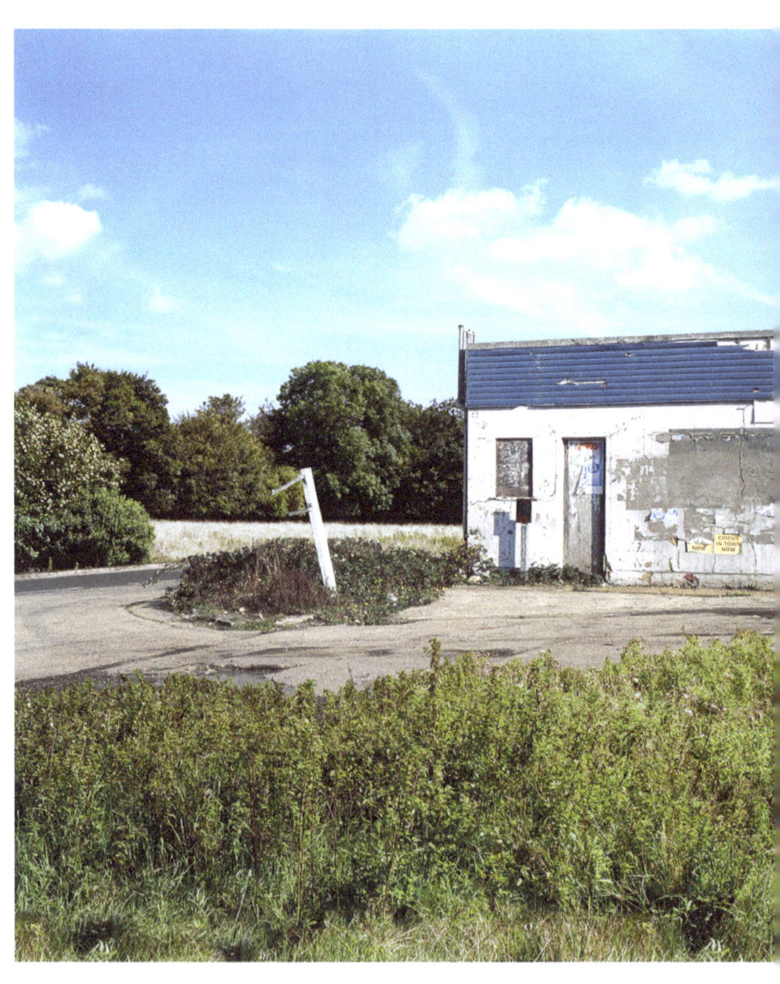

Landscape with Ruin III (2006)
from the series *Landscape with Ruin*

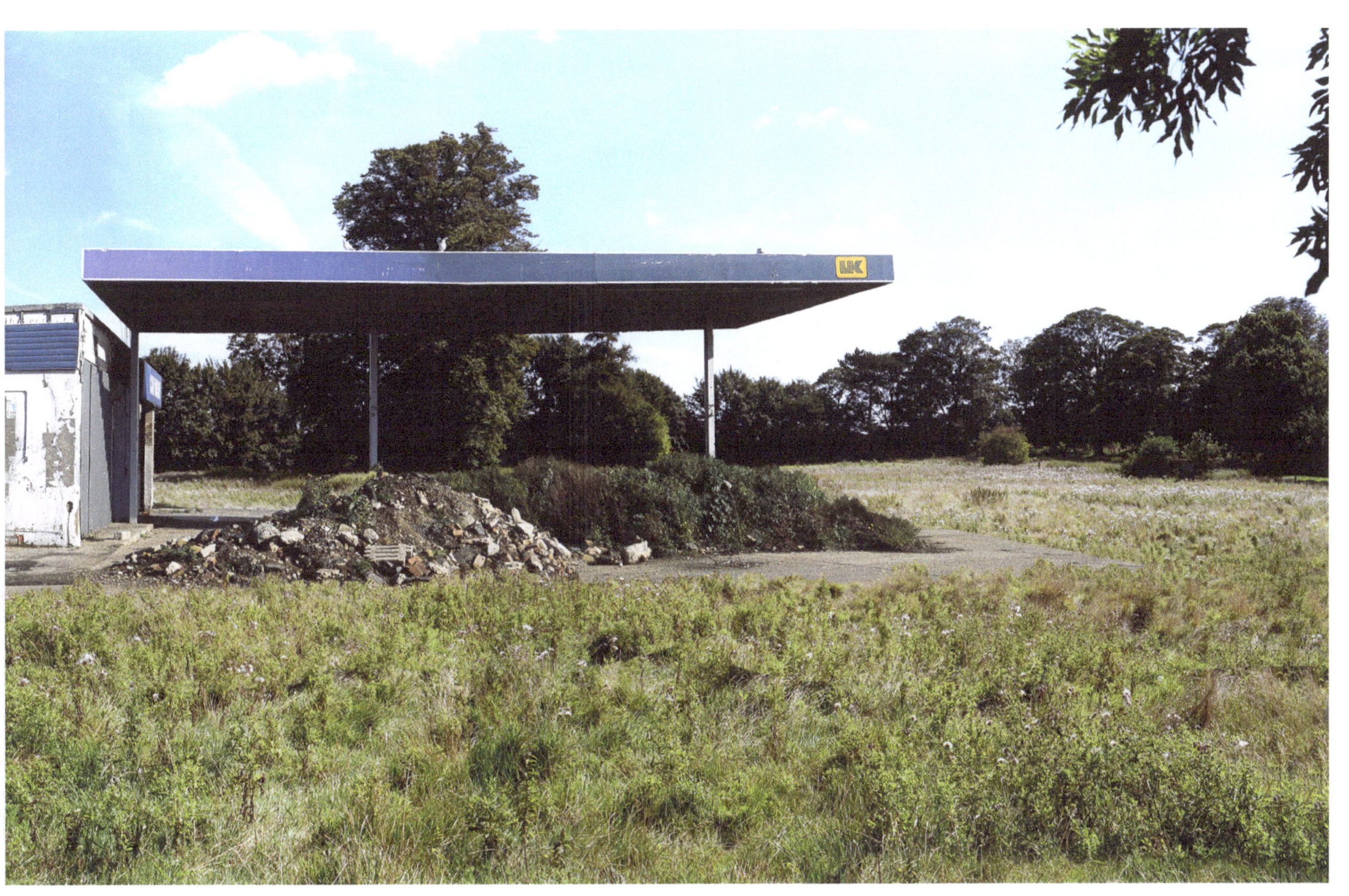

ЛК

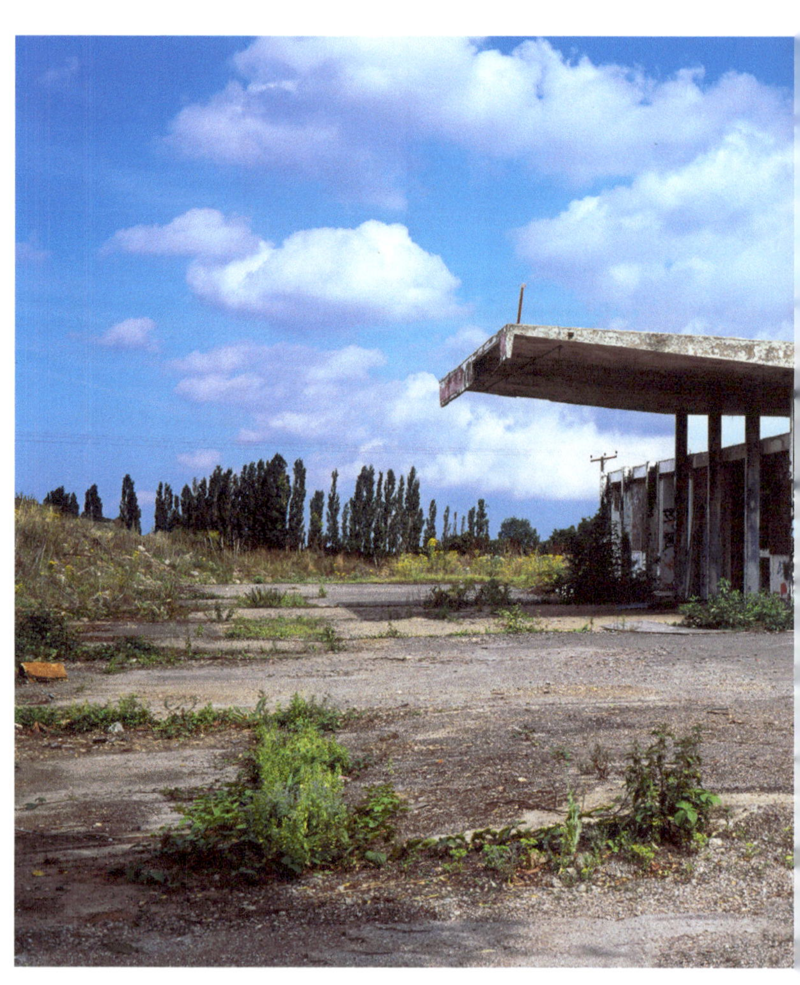

Landscape with Ruin VIII (2005)
from the series *Landscape with Ruin*

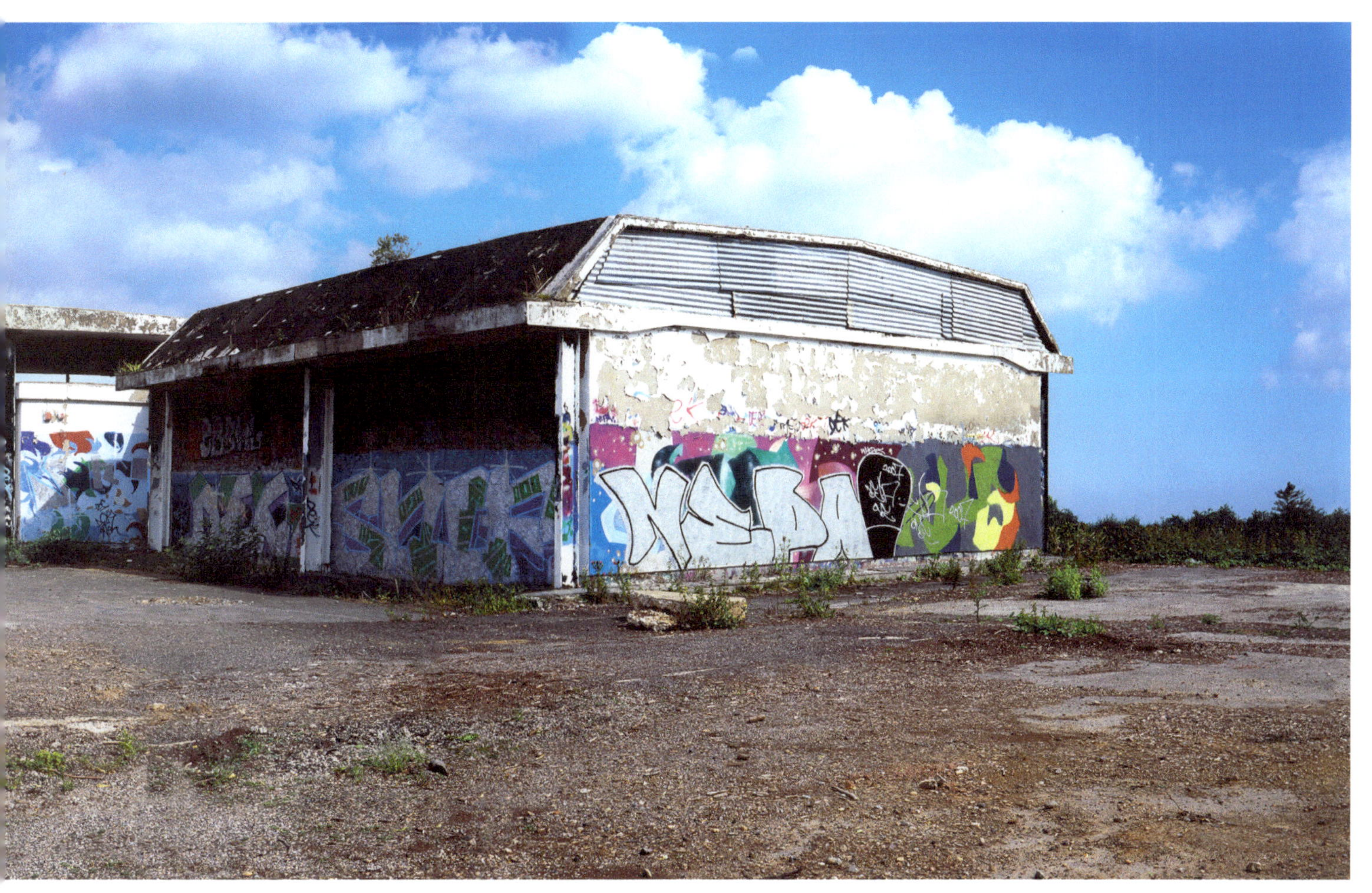

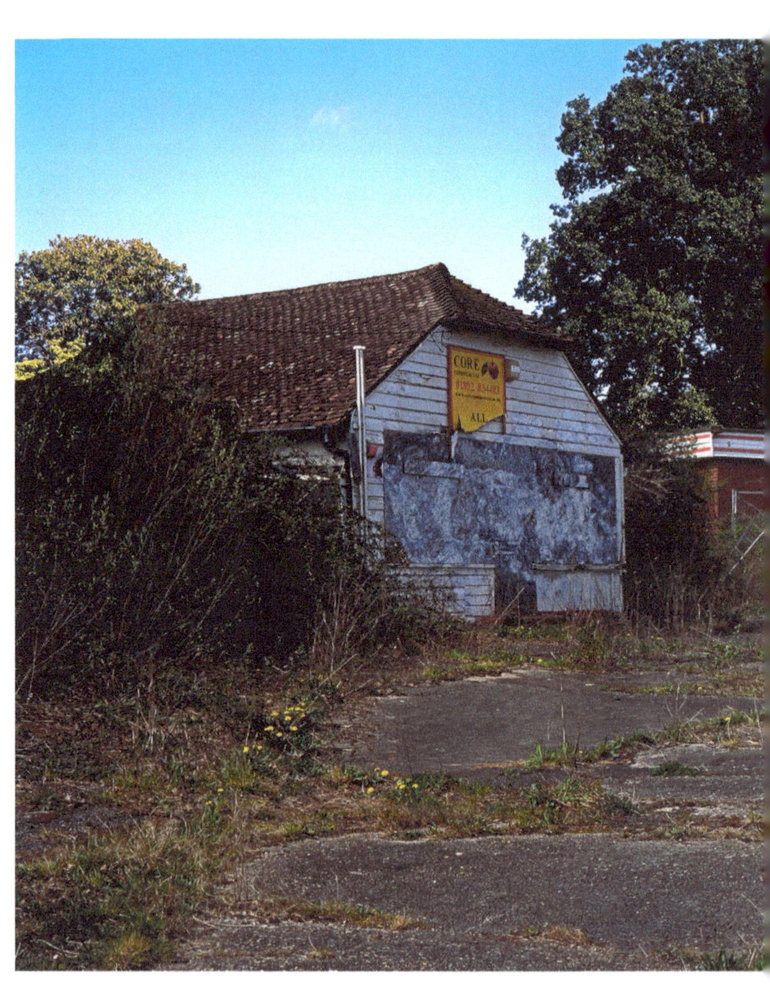

Landscape with Ruin IX (2006)
from the series *Landscape with Ruin*

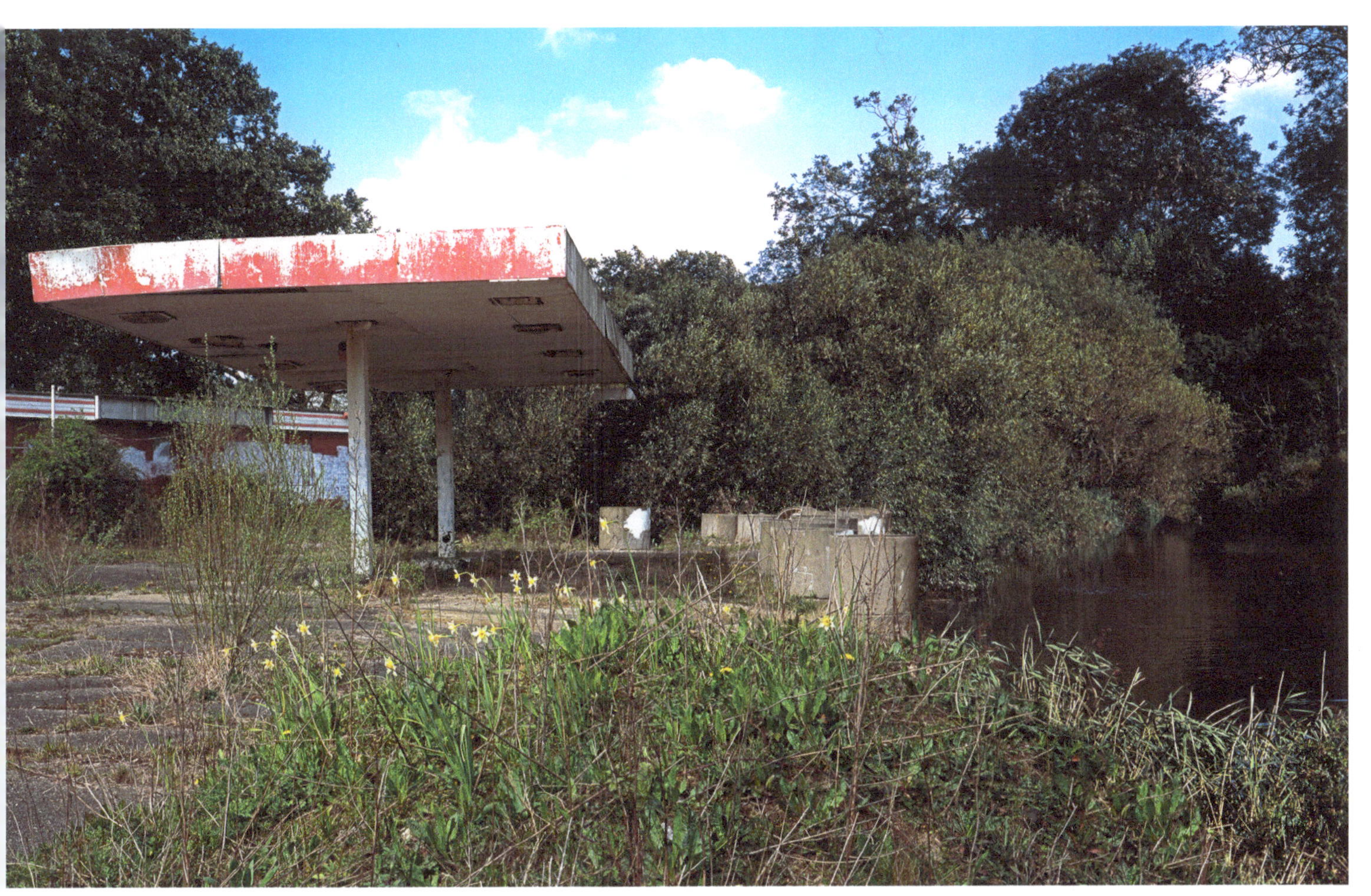

Initially, the series *And Then There Were None* seems to concern itself entirely with interior space; there seems to be no trace of the concern with landscape that characterised much of the earlier work. Closer consideration, however, reveals that a reflection on landscape does still exist through its reference to the Picturesque and its exploration of the vantage point from which the Picturesque landscape might be viewed.

Emerging in the 18th century, the aesthetic principle of the Picturesque was defined by its pursuit of a wilder, more rugged depiction of nature, a depiction that was found to exist in the work of painters such as Claude Lorrain. One aspect of this treatment of nature was the roughened textures of aged and weathered surfaces. The early followers of the Picturesque held that an appreciation of the textures of age and decay was not confined to those found in gnarled oaks and ancient ruins; the textures of decay manifest in the lives of the rural poor were found equally appealing. The craggy faces of those eking out a living, cottages and hovels in disrepair, lives unaffected by modern day improvement, were all recognised as having aesthetic value. It could be said that the Picturesque aesthetic, in one form at least, found its meaning through inequities of power. Advocates of the Picturesque were typically those who were in a position to enjoy the pastoral landscape at a distance rather than those who knew it at close quarters and worked the land through necessity.

Compositional conventions in the Picturesque, and the placing of the viewer in an ideal position to recognise the scene as a coherent whole, assisted this sense of empowerment. The naturalism of the scene, its seemingly unstructured appearance, helped to create a sense of mastery and omniscience, since the 'randomness' of the scene 'hides' the vantage point from which the viewer is able to see with perfect clarity. Landscapes with this kind of disorderly order are are in fact completed by the viewer's presence. The viewer's look fills the gap in the geometry of the picture; the scene anticipates the spectator and subjugates itself to the spectator's look. Yet, in that this feeling of empowerment is achieved through the viewer adopting a given vantage point, the Picturesque, like the trompe l'oeil, offers a fragile position of mastery. Rather than situating the spectator in a position where some true essence of nature is revealed, the Picturesque could be regarded as merely appeasing a desire for nature to be a certain way; we are perhaps offered the illusion that nature is not indifferent to our existence.

Lacan's notion of the returned gaze is of relevance here, with the subject's sense of self being influenced by the external world. At the heart of the Picturesque, it could be said, is a desire for nature to counter a lack by substantiating the viewer's sense of relationship with the world. The frame and pictorial conventions are a hindrance to this since they potentially reveal the artifice of the construction. For this reason the viewer must deny the frame's existence as a curtailing perimeter. The composition must rest easily within its boundary. The vantage point on the Picturesque scene could thus be viewed as a site of conflict where a desire for wholeness - the self embedded in nature - necessitates a denial of the formal elements of construction.

In the series *And Then There Were None,* the country house is used to represent this site of conflict. Country houses in the 18th century began to be built on higher ground to take fuller advantage of the views of the gardens, which increasingly were being modelled in the Picturesque style. In this way, the country house became the focal point of the surrounding 'naturalised' landscapes with all views facing towards a vantage point occupied by the house and its inhabitants. In the series, the landscape beyond the room is seldom seen. The focus is on the landscape we imagine to be there. Although we do catch sight of it here and there, and its presence is expressed through artifacts within the rooms, we are, in the main, denied any confirmation that we occupy the vantage point. We are in a state of limbo where the landscape seems close to laying itself before us but in most cases it is merely the light that streams through

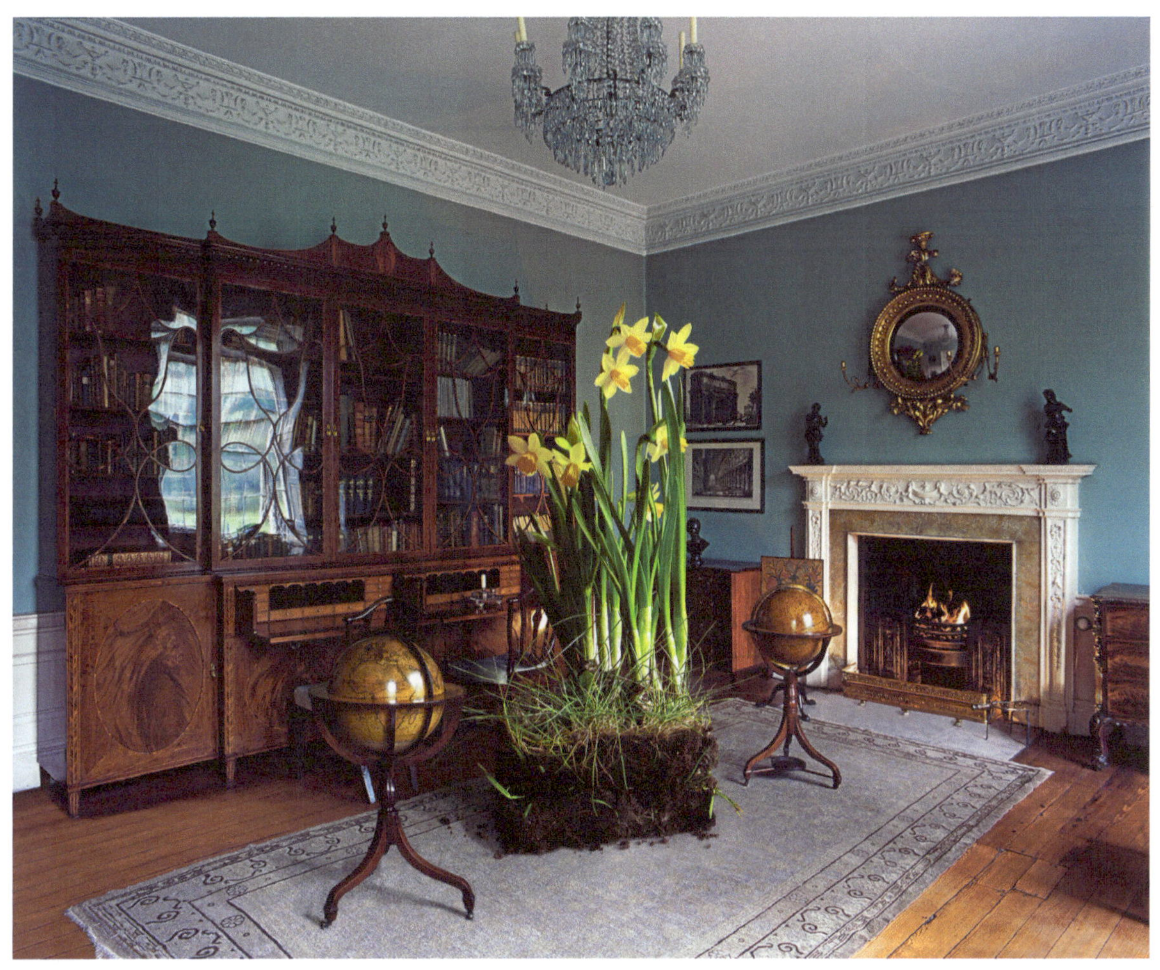

Study with Daffodils (2010)
from the series *And Then There Were None*

the windows that gives us a tantalising sense of the exterior space.

The pervading tone of disquiet in the work can be linked not just to the struggle for a sense of self but also to the histories associated with the interiors themselves. Social inequalities and injustices, it could be said, are woven into the fabric of many English country houses, not least for the associations many have with the profits from imperial conquest and slavery. Yet, in the absence of the Picturesque view, and the sense of empowerment this might provide, the rooms themselves seem to elevate our status. The heritage interiors offer a familiar trope of Englishness, and this world, external to the self, seems to confer subjecthood upon us.

The large, collaged objects that appear in the rooms, however, introduce a presence that is spectral and uncanny. The comfort afforded by the heritage interior is challenged. Thus the site of conflict is one in which the spectator recognises the affirmation of self on offer but is required to navigate around the evidence of construction, bypassing the signs that might destabalise the privileged position that is otherwise available. In *Ballroom with Milking Stool* (2008) we feel ourselves to be in a space that is part of the tradition of the English social elite. The tall Georgian window, the wood-panelling and large hanging tapestry are some of the indicators that suggest this. Through the window we can see distant trees and can gauge the extent of the grounds that surround the house. There is a stillness both inside and out: nothing stirs in the grounds and the piano in the room with its closed lid seems to emphasise the silence. The only figures we see are those in the tapestry that form part of some kind of celebration of nature. It is difficult to make a judgment on the period that is represented. The interior has a timelessness that denies any easy reading of tell-tale signs. There is a feeling that time has stood still and that such spaces are a refuge from the troubles and uncertainties of the modern world. Without knowing the title, we might initially be confused by the large three-legged piece of furniture that seems unusually worn. We might at first mistake it for some kind of crudely fashioned table. Once we realise it is a stool, its unrealistic size begins to undermine the authority of the stately interior.

Imagining life in the country house in the past we might be forgiven for dwelling on the idea of a life of leisure and privilege. The class divisions that would have played a part in providing this we may feel we are able to justify on the basis that, so we understand it, harmony across the classes generally prevailed; that the deference shown by the servant class was reciprocated by the paternalistic care of the 'master'. But the presence of the milking stool seems to contradict this version of the past. The deeply worn texture of the stool ought to bring Picturesque appeal as its weathered surface should put us in mind of the charms of rustic life, but the stark contrast between it and the more refined wooden structures in the room instead make us think of the life of labour to which it was attached.

Lacan's analysis of Holbein's painting *The Ambassadors* (1533) considers the way in which an anamorphic skull in the painting undermines the spectator's mastery of the scene.[1] The portrait of two world travellers and their possessions allows the spectator standing before the painting to assume the subject position, at first, without contradiction. But the eventual recognition of the skull from an altered viewpoint pulls the rug from under the subject's feet by revealing the void that has opened up where the spectator once stood. The spectator, now defined by the painting, becomes the object of a returned gaze. Holbein's memento mori, for Lacan, represents the collapse of subjecthood that occurs when the viewer is no longer addressed by the reality of the picture. Dispossessed of their vantage point, the world is seen differently; the viewer is no longer attuned to or beckoned by the coded display of symbols that constitiute the culture of linguistic meaning. Slavov Zizek, in his book *Looking Awry*, imagines the moment when the viewer of *The Ambassadors* takes a final look back towards the painting and, noticing the skull, finds the true meaning of the picture to then be disclosed, namely 'the nullity of all terrestrial goods, objects of art and knowledge that fill out the rest of the picture.'[2] At this point, the resolved gratification from the riches displayed begins to untangle, 'rendering all its constituents "suspicious," and opening up 'the abyss of the search for meaning.'

In the series *And Then There Were None* there are no such anamorphic devices. But in images such as *Study with Daffodils* (2007) there is a similar intervening presence that unsteadies the viewer's engagement with the 'riches' presented. A reminder of Holbein's painting is detectable in that, within the floor space, two large globes offer a similar signification of discovery and conquest as that found in *The Ambassadors*. Between them the daffodils of the title stand erect – their placement between the two globes taking on an obvious phallic suggestion. Whilst the daffodils might initially be thought to enhance the romanticist connotations of the work, this is counterd by the fact that they have been roughly lifted from the ground, the sod of earth and scattered particles of soil coveying a more visceral and immediate manipulation of land than one would normally associate with a romantic sensibility. As a consequence, the authority of the presiding order seems unstable and contestable.

In *Ballroom with Milking Stool,* and others in the series, we might say that something similar is in operation. The collaged objects conform to the perspective of the space in which they are situated, and appear to share the same light source, but their presence interrupts the viewer's complicity with the narrative of tradition and heritage that would otherwise draw us in. The stool, through its crude, functional form, fractures the 'memory' of the past. History becomes histories. The spectator can no longer rely upon the 'authenticity' of the room (many are displays within museums) to adopt a position of subjecthood. Just as the spectator's vision of the external world must steer clear of contradiction for subjectivity to be affirmed, the interruption of the givenness of the room's appearance reduces its potential for

conferring a sense of belonging on the viewer.

In other images, we find objects that similarly threaten to topple the spectator's subject position. Often this threat may not be immediately realised as the objects themselves offer visual delight and a fetishistic pleasure in the historical artefact – an antique silver coffee pot, an 'Uncle Tom' Staffordshire figurine. But as clues they can be unpicked, and the narrative dimension that begins to come to mind when considering the series as a whole is that of the country house 'whodunit'. Here, however, we are invited to detect crimes and injustices in which we may ourselves be implicated. The subjecthood on offer is caught up within a discourse of power and privilege but to unravel this and interrogate the specular image of wholeness we may uncover our own vested interests and our own vulnerabilities.

Notes

1. Lacan, J. (1979) The Four Fundamental Concepts of Psycho-analysis, London: Penguin Books, pp. 86–89.

2. Zizek, S. (1992) Looking Awry: An Introduction to Jacques Lacan Through Popular Culture, Cambridge: Mass, MIT Press, pp. 90–91.

Breakfast Room with Pail (2011)
from the series *And Then There Were None*

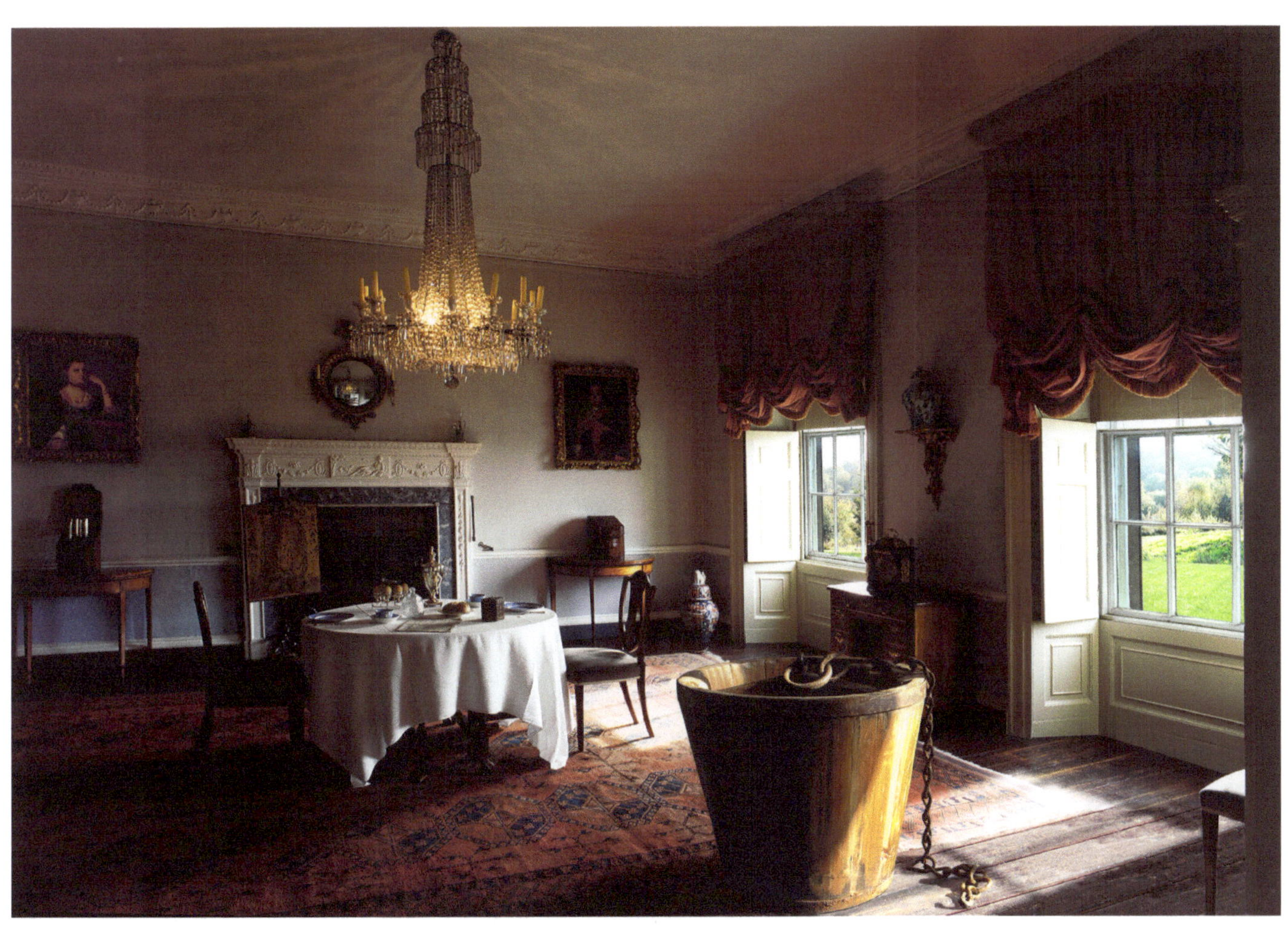

Bedroom with Wooden Figure (2012)
from the series *And Then There Were None*

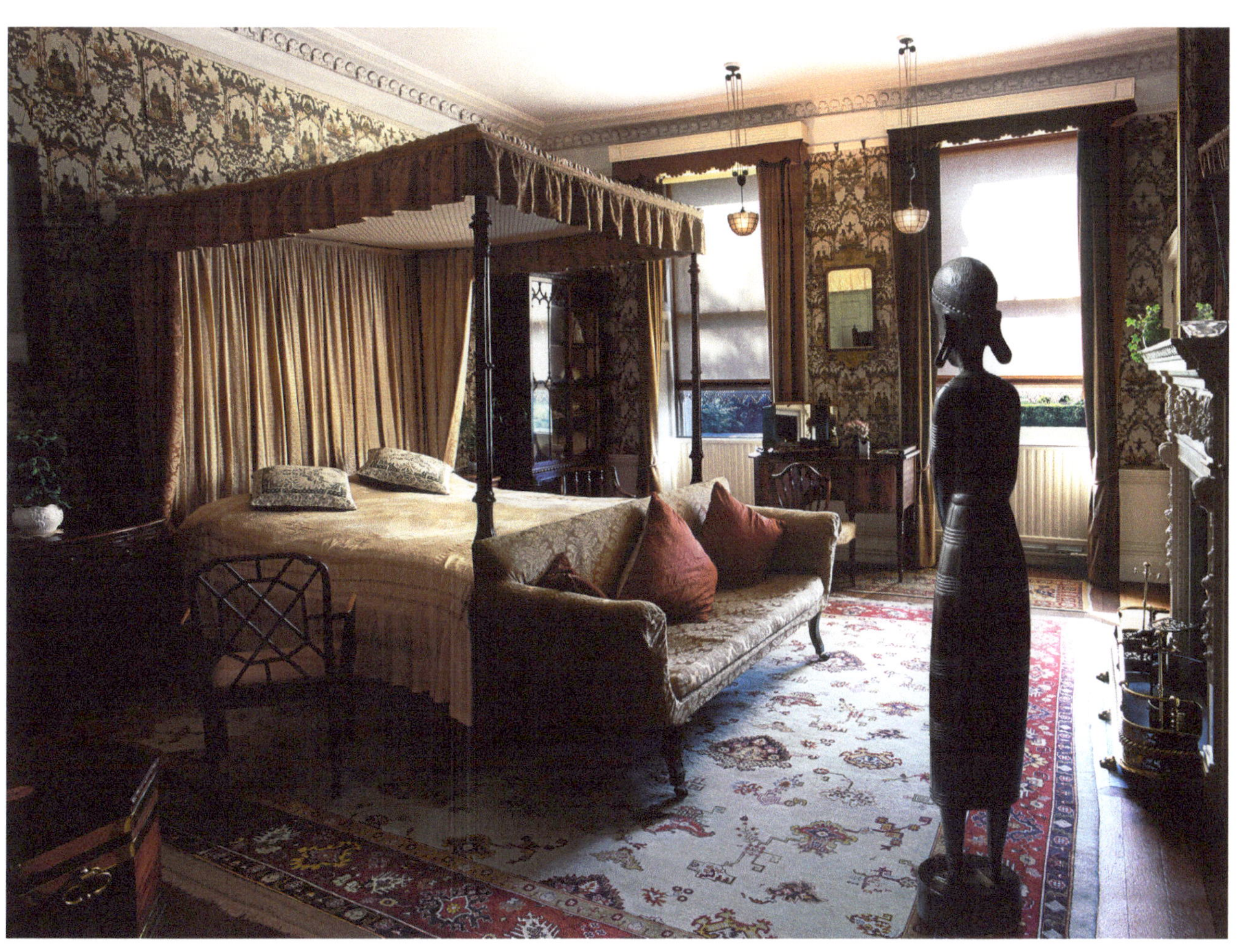

Bedroom with Scissors (2009)
from the series *And Then There Were None*

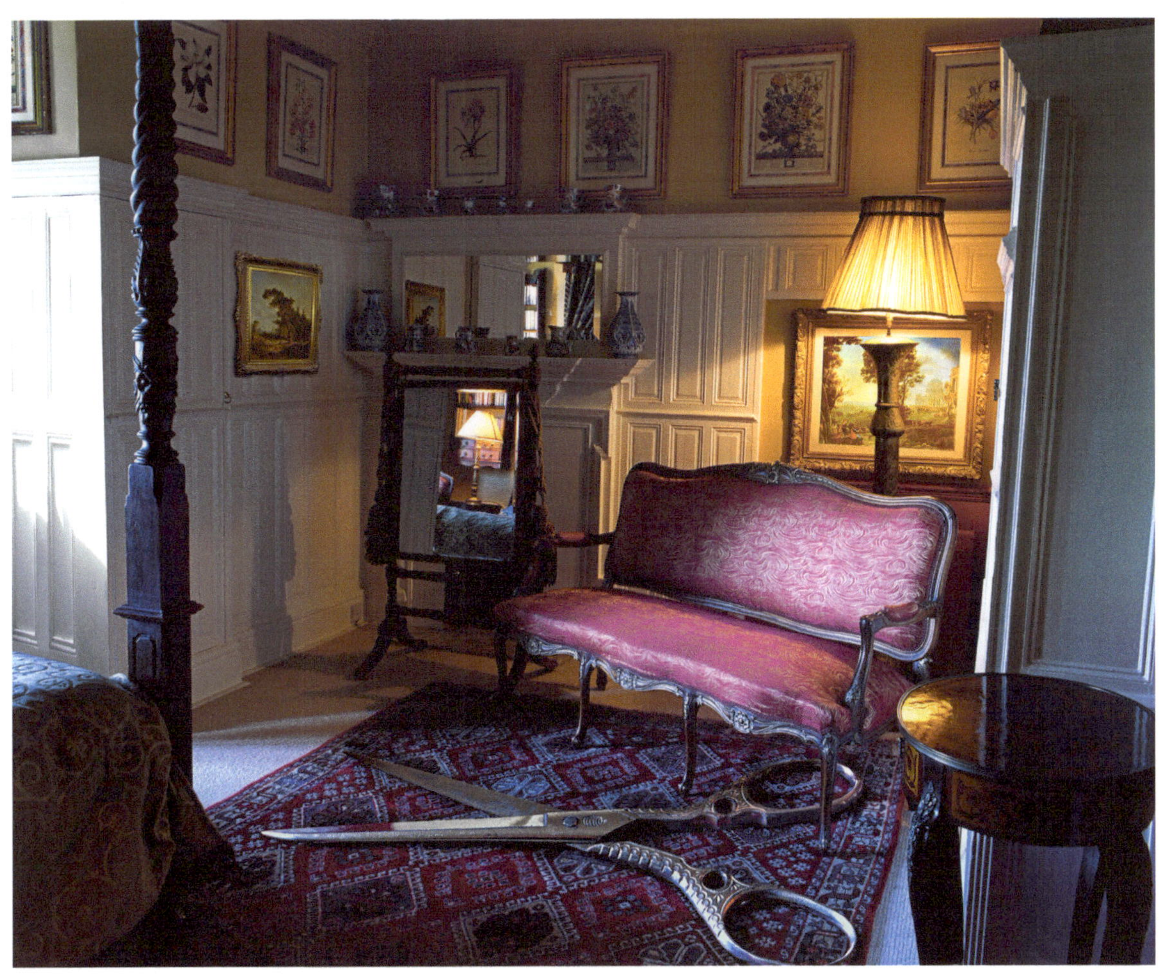

Drawing Room with Pheasant (2010)
from the series *And Then There Were None*

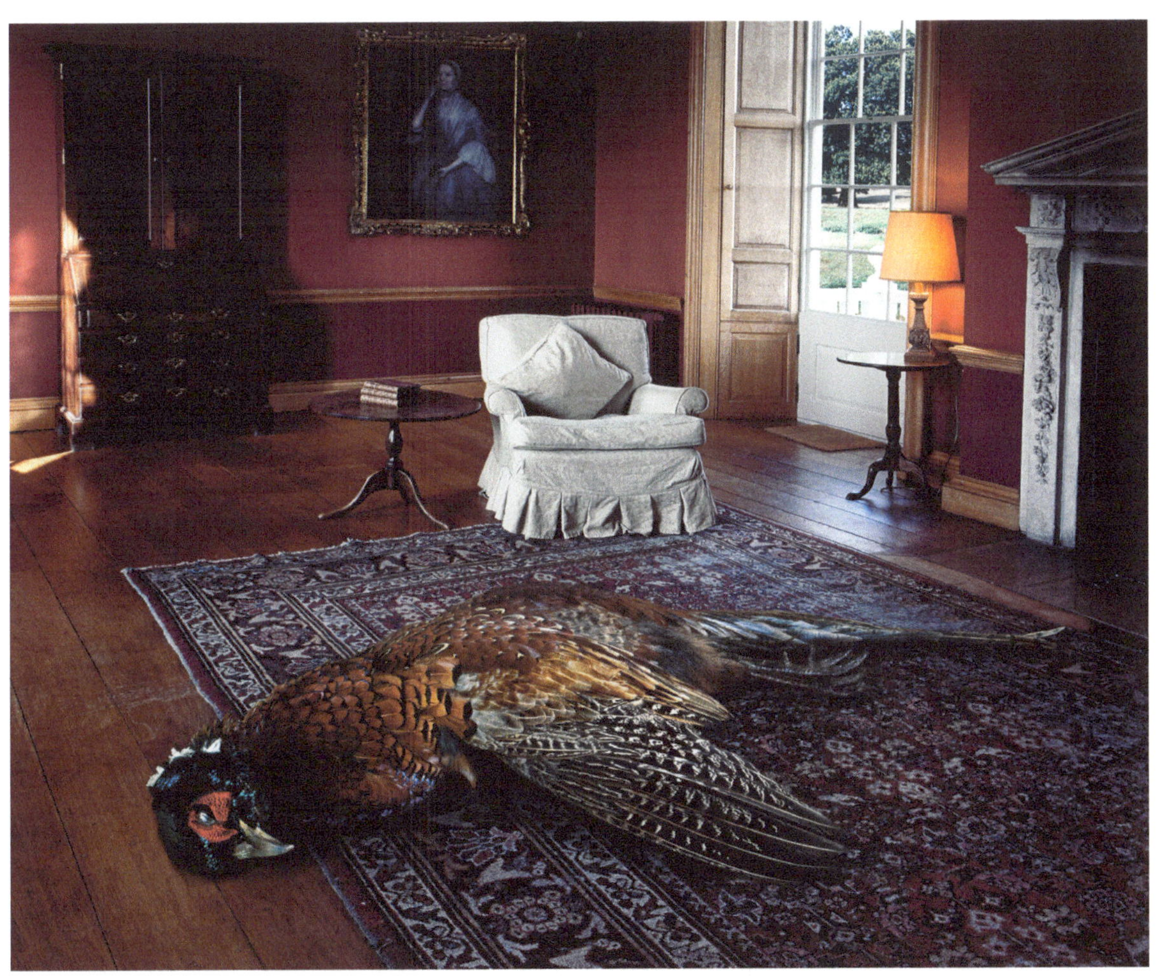

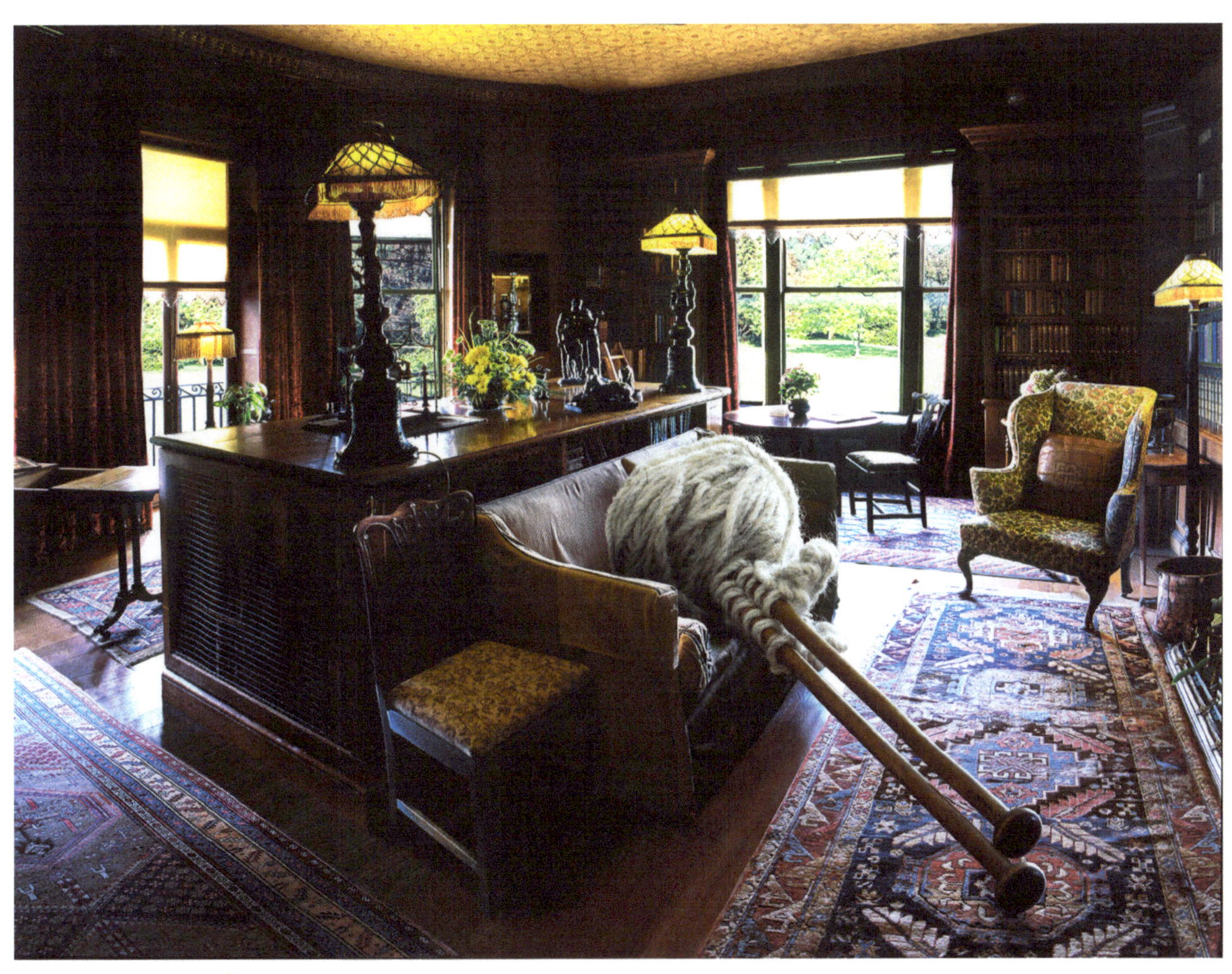

Drawing Room with Playing Cards (2010)
from the series And Then There Were None

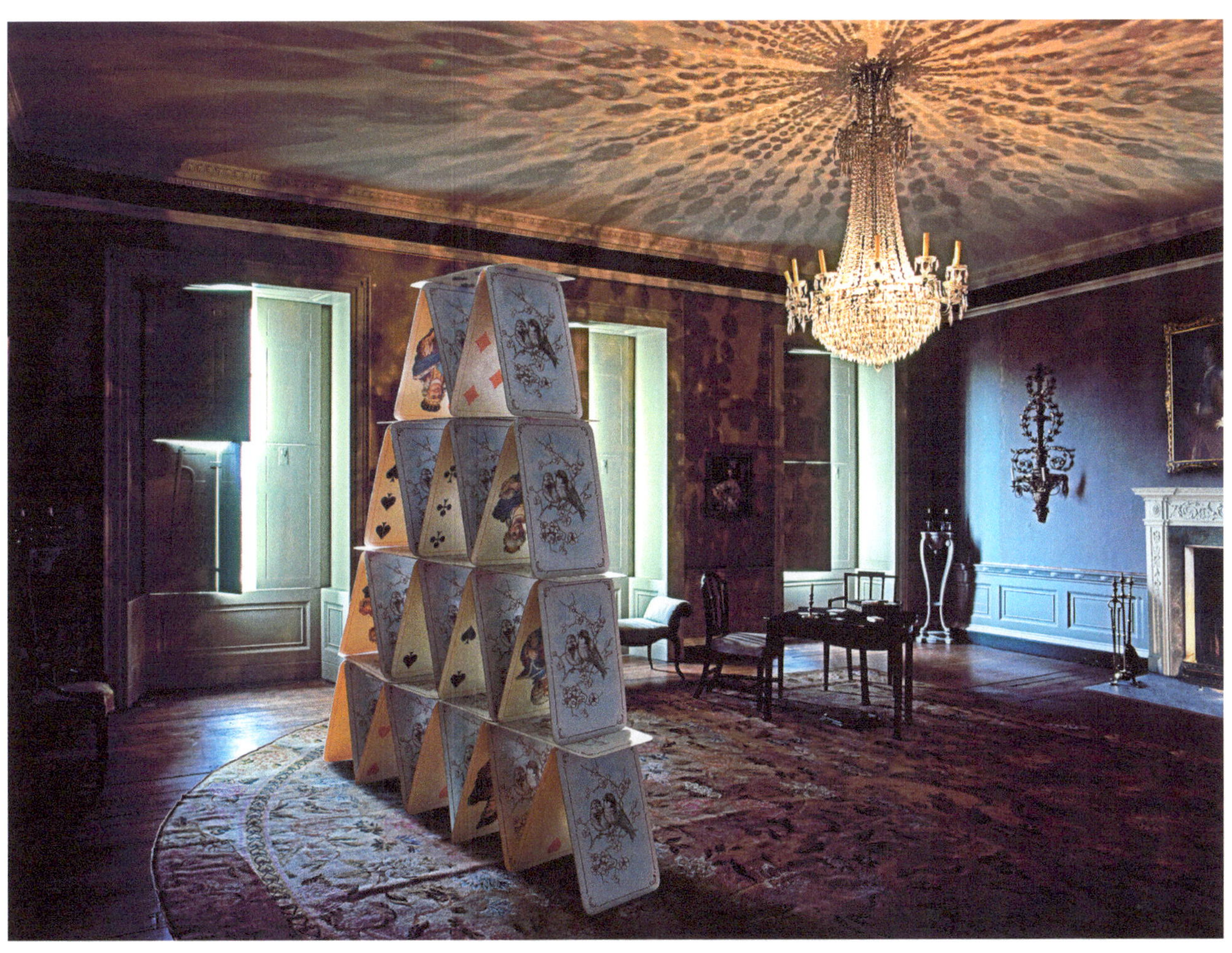

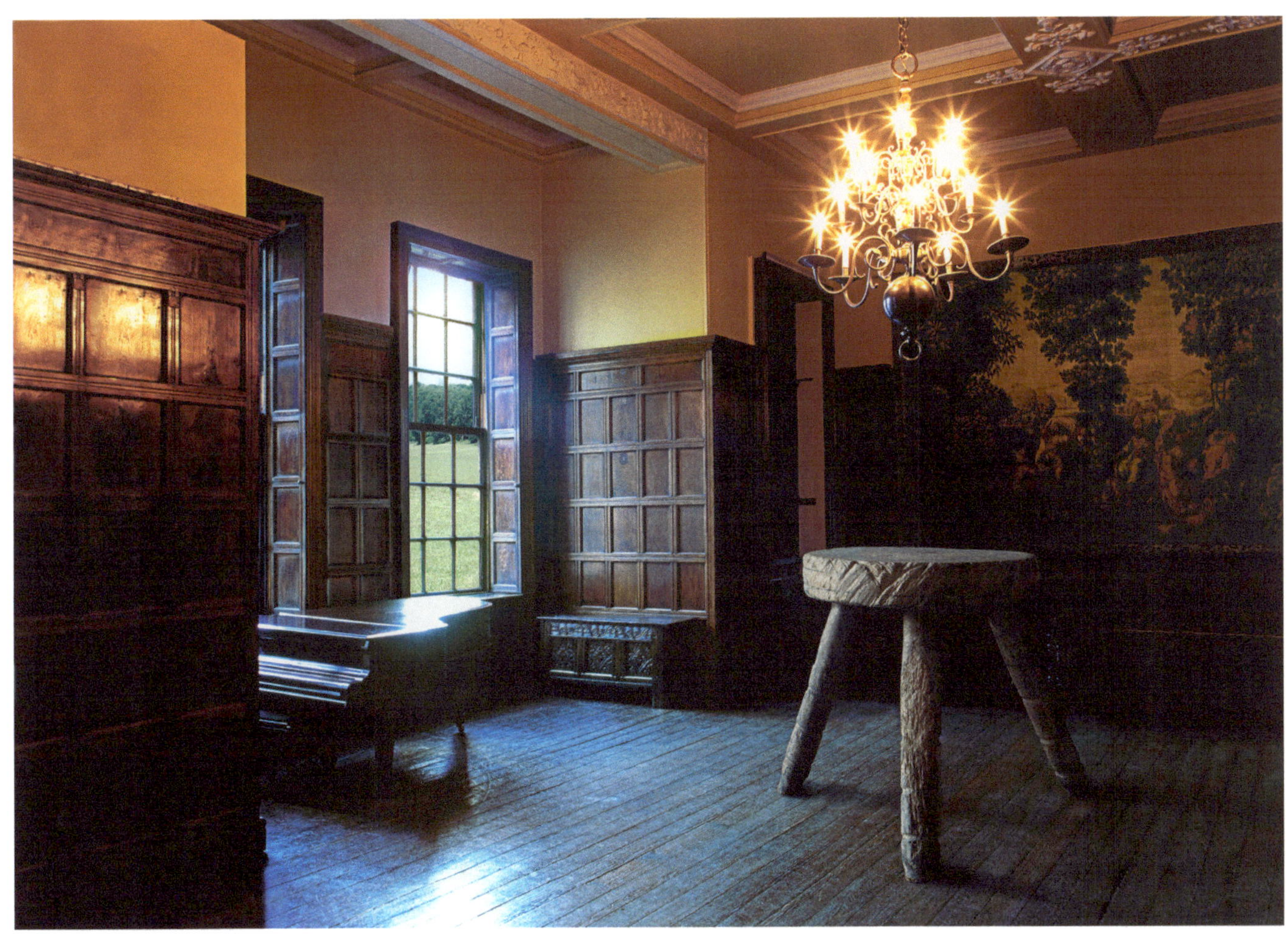

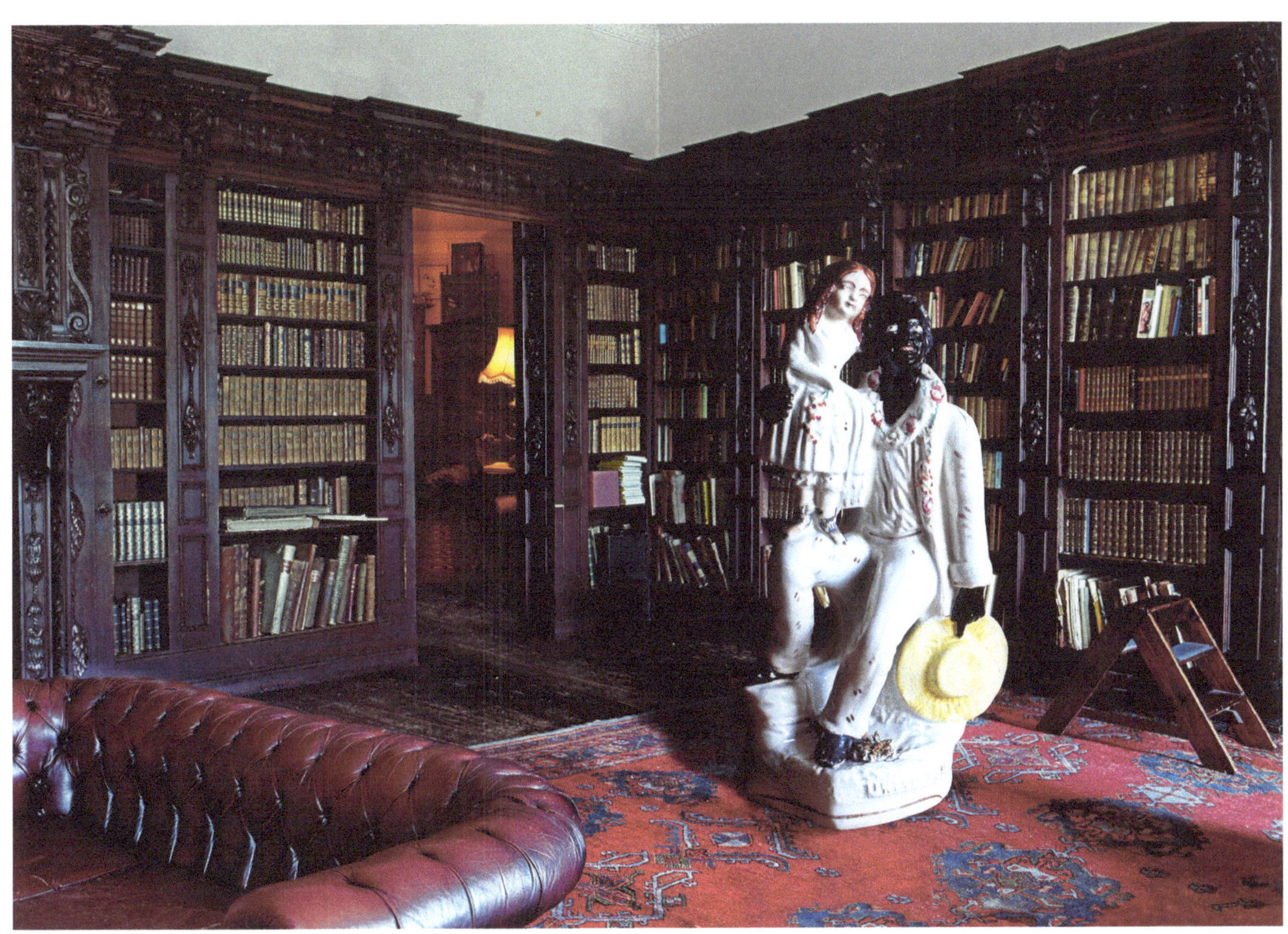

Hallway with Coffee Pot (2011)
from the series *And Then There Were None*

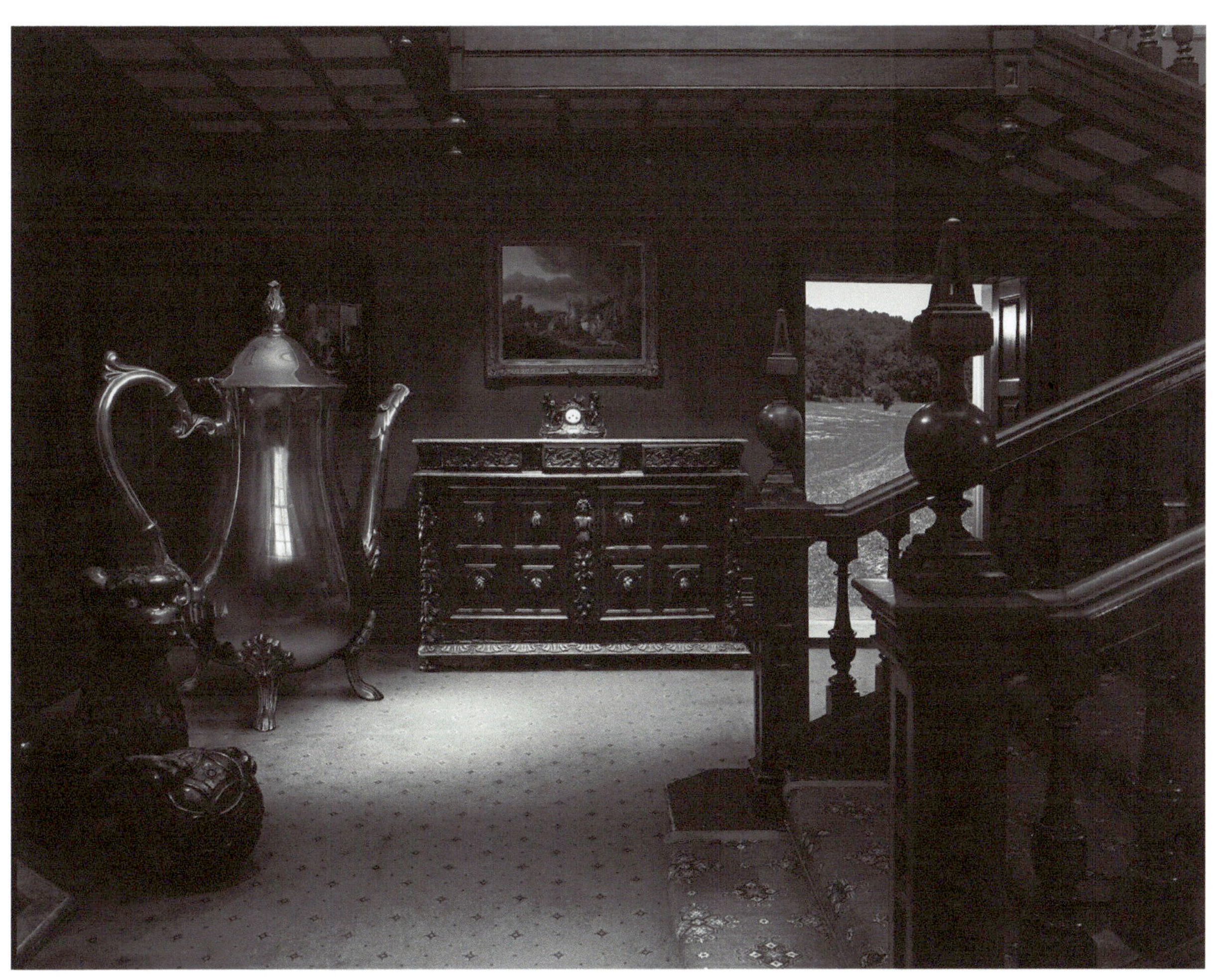

Billiards Room with Rope (2009)
from the series *And Then There Were None*

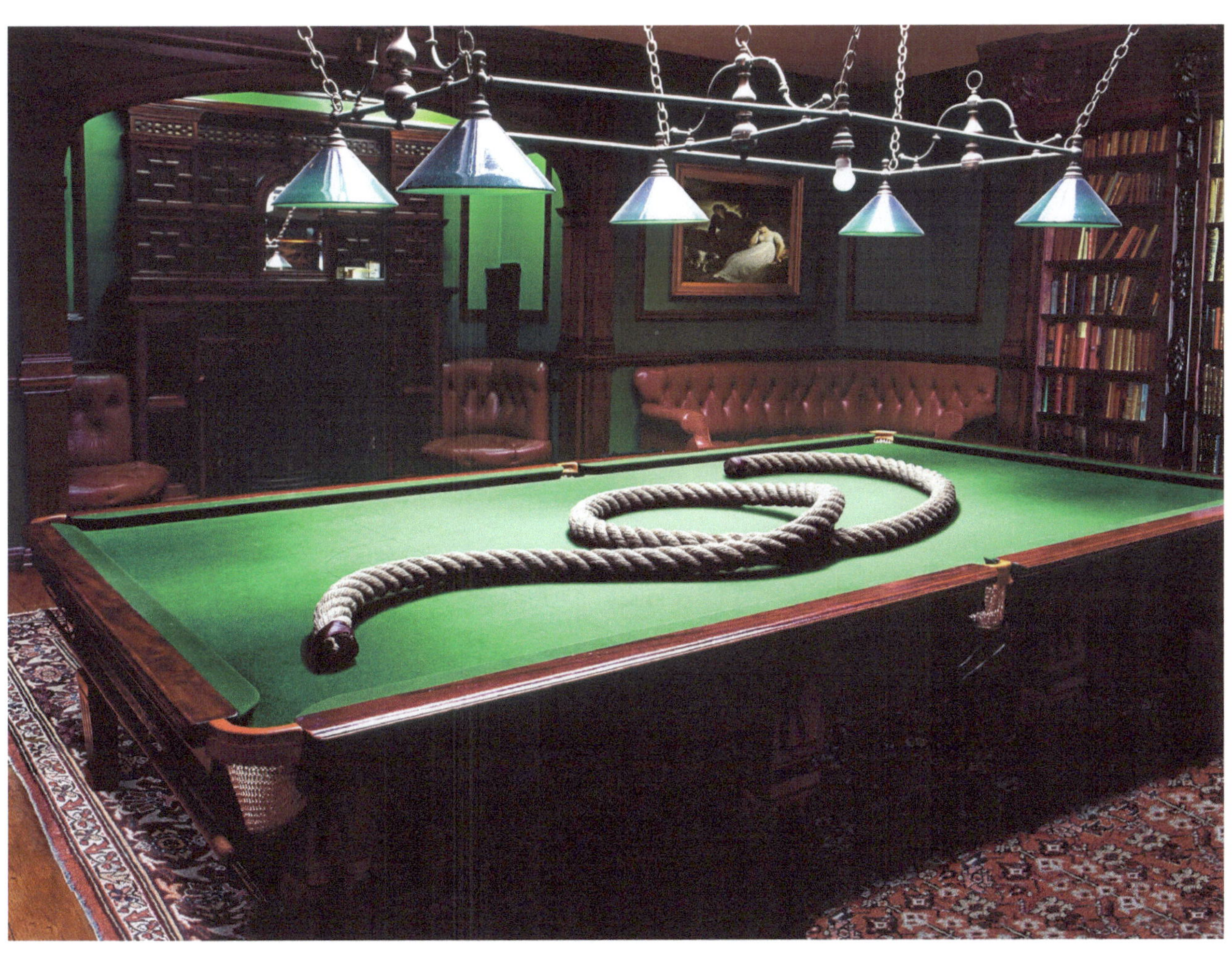

Boudoir with Gun (2012)
from the series *And Then There Were None*

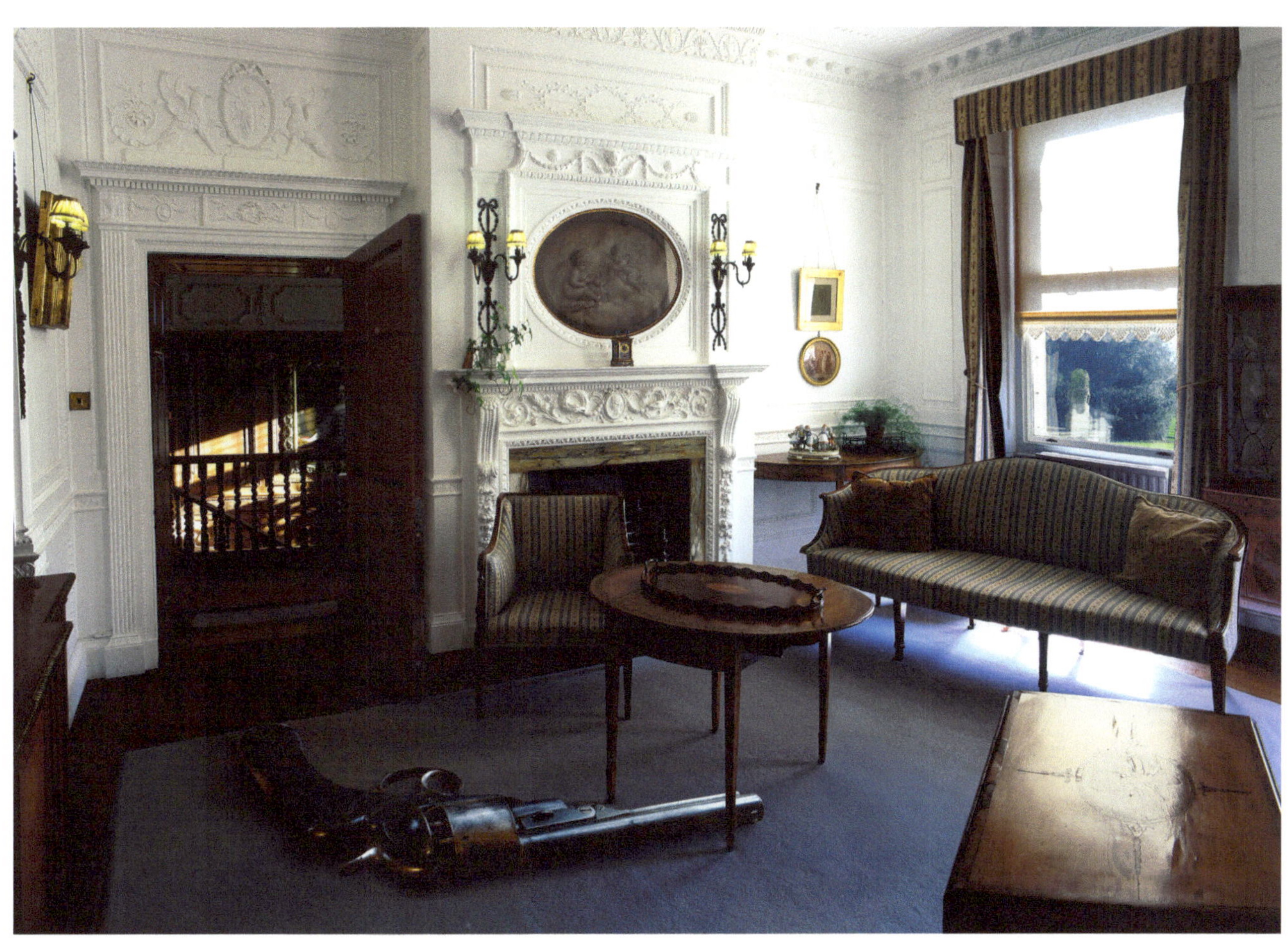